FAITH
SHAPING

FAITH SHAPING

Stephen D. Jones

NURTURING THE FAITH JOURNEY OF YOUTH

Judson Press ® Valley Forge

Faith Shaping

Copyright © 1980
Judson Press, Valley Forge, PA 19481

Unless otherwise indicated, Bible quotations in this volume are from the Revised Standard Version of the Bible, copyrighted 1946, 1952, 1971, 1973 © by the Division of Christian Education of the National Council of the Churches of Christ in the United States of America, and are used by permission.

Other versions of the Bible quoted in this book are:

The New Testament in Modern English, rev. ed. Copyright © J. B. Phillips 1972. Used by permission of The Macmillan Company and Geoffrey Bles, Ltd.

Today's English Version, the *Good News Bible*—Old Testament: Copyright © American Bible Society, 1976; New Testament: Copyright © American Bible Society 1966, 1971, 1976.

The New English Bible, Copyright © The Delegates of the Oxford University Press and The Syndics of the Cambridge University Press, 1961, 1970.

The Holy Bible, King James Version.

Library of Congress Cataloging in Publication Data
Jones, Stephen D.
   Faith shaping.
   Includes bibliographical references.
    1. Youth—Religious life.   2. Church work with
youth.   I. Title.
BV4531.2.J64   268'.433   80-19733
ISBN 0-8170-0915-9

Contents

Preface   7
Chapters
   1. The Shape of Faith Nurturing Today   11
   2. The Act of Welcoming   27
   3. Memorable Faith   35
   4. Faith Shaping: How Youth Acquire Faith   43
   5. Basics and Beginnings   63
   6. Giftedness: A Unique Faith-Shaping Agenda   71
   7. Contexts for Faith Nurturing   79
   8. Practices and Proposals   95
   9. A Person of Christian Faith   111
   10. A New Mandate!   125
Appendix   129

Preface

My Motivation

I was certainly one of the lucky ones. I had two caring parents who had both an expressive and sophisticated faith. They were intentional in nurturing faith in our home and in our involvement with the church.

I was surrounded within that church by a smaller cell of ten families who fellowshipped, recreated, celebrated, and uplifted faith together. I could turn to these two handfuls of adults for Christian love and support, even when I did nothing to deserve it. I participated in a church that allowed me to use my leadership skills in a significant position as a senior high young person.

Those years were the 1950s and early 1960s, when values were more homogenous. That place, also, was a small town in rural mid-America at a time when society was a closer-knit circle. Almost everything in my life reinforced my faith. The first challenge, from a public school teacher, came at the right time to spur additional faith growth. I then attended a church-related college in which alternative models of Christian faith were readily available.

Most young persons are not so lucky. From my own heritage of faith, I am motivated to do something to help faith nurturing of adolescents in what is admittedly a much more difficult era.

My Audience: A Faith-Nurturing Team

In this book I will advocate adolescent faith nurturing as an effort to be undertaken by the self, by peers, and by a variety of adults. Nurturing of any kind is rarely a solo performance. We must recognize that it requires an entire team of concerned persons. The best faith nurturing will occur when church youth sponsors, leaders, pastors, teachers, parents, adult friends, and peers provide together a supportive environment for personal growth and faith development. It is to all of these participants in the faith nurturing team that this book is addressed.

My Perspective: A Local Church Pastor and Educator

I have been privileged to serve in two exciting churches as team pastor, in which I shared with another leader the pastoral responsibilities. This relationship allowed me to emphasize, along with other priorities, a ministry with youth. I realized early in my experience that ministry with youth means much more than working with the youth groups and classes. Perhaps most importantly, it involves coordinating and guiding a church's faith development emphasis. "Our conviction is that the process of faith development ought to be the actual primary task of the church."[1]

My professional training as a Christian educator has helped me understand the special needs of youth and young adults. I hope that my perspective as both pastor and educator is evident in these pages.

My Subject: Adolescents

The adolescent years may be the most puzzling for adults to understand. Adolescents themselves are often confused about what they are experiencing and feeling. It is no insult to call them "in-between" or transitional years. These are the journey years through which a child becomes an adult.

Because these are in-between years does not imply that they are a developmental lull.

[1] James D. Anderson and Ezra Earl Jones, *The Management of Ministry* (New York: Harper & Row, Publishers, Inc., 1978), p. 125.

Man is distinguished from the lower animals by growing up twice. The latter pass from birth to maturity in one smooth sweep of growth, but man's development is interrupted. In childhood a certain degree of maturity is reached, but this is broken up by the great upheaval—bodily, mentally, emotionally—of adolescence. Thus there is closer affinity between childhood and adulthood than between childhood and adolescence or between childhood and infancy. Adolescence is a kind of second infancy, in which development is rapid as in the first infancy and there is a similar richness of imagination and fantasy. Childhood, on the other hand, is a period of stability and toughness, a period of consolidation rather than of change.[2]

Adolescence and young adulthood are among the most active developmental years when life-changing directions are established. Major personality changes are experienced. Independence is gained. Values and morals are claimed. Personhood is expressed. And perhaps most importantly, faith is shaped.

I will, in some sections of this book, talk about the childhood years because they are the foundation upon which the adolescent years are built. But I will most carefully explore adolescence. The years of young adulthood (often considered to begin with high school graduation) are difficult to distinguish developmentally because they are an outgrowth of adolescence. I will consider the tasks of shaping faith, and it is during adolescence and young adulthood that these tasks are most actively explored.

My Style

If you are looking for a new program idea for your youth group, you are reading the wrong book. It is true that there are practical ideas in the latter chapters, but they are not ready-made programs.

The first chapter explores the two primary problems that we face in adolescent faith nurturing and introduces my approach. The second and third chapters discuss the adult responsibilities in providing a context for faith development with youth. Chapter 4 explores the faith-shaping tasks, or how youth acquire faith. Chapter 5 talks about the necessary foundations during the childhood years. Chapter 6 lifts up the important faith-shaping concern of helping youth explore their gifts and potential. In chapters 7 and 8 the practical concerns of faith nurturing with adolescents are approached from two different perspec-

[2]R. S. Lee, *Your Growing Child and Religion* (New York: Macmillan, Inc., 1963), p. 195. © Roy S. Lee, 1963.

tives. Chapter 9 is a theological undergirding which describes a person of mature Christian faith. While we recognize that everyone develops faith, the particular quality, content, depth, and direction of a person's faith are our concern here. Finally, chapter 10 articulates a biblical mandate for nurturing youth as they shape a personal faith.

My Debt

This book was written out of work done on a Faith Development Component as a part of a National Strategy for Youth Ministry which was developed by the Department of Ministry with Youth of the Board of Educational Ministries, American Baptist Churches in the U.S.A. The intent of this National Strategy is to develop new directions and to plow creative ground in ministry with youth in the coming years. The faith development component is one undergirding aspect of this thrust by American Baptists.

I owe a word of debt to the American Baptist Churches' Department of Ministry with Youth for their support in this project. Particularly am I grateful to John "Bud" Carroll for his creative guidance as this book unfolded from embryonic to completed stage.

The two churches I have served have been exciting arenas in which to learn and grow in ministry with youth. My debt to the First Baptist Churches of Dayton, Ohio, and Boulder, Colorado, runs deep, as both of them have taught me more than I could possibly have otherwise learned.

For some reason, I write and think best after midnight; so most of this book was written in the early hours of the morning. I am most appreciative of my wife, Jan, who encourages me and grants me the freedom to pursue this erratic life-style.

Chapter 1

The Shape
of
Faith Nurturing
Today

*The day has come for an entirely new level of consciousness
and intentionality regarding adolescent faith nurturing in the
church and home. Underneath, if not on the surface, young
persons are pleading for help in facing life's ultimate, and
therefore most important, questions. If faith is life's foundation, then we had best help youth build it before we worry
a great deal with the appearance of the structure.*

FAITH: a personal answer to the question, "Where do I place
    my ultimate trust?"
FAITH NURTURING: all efforts to pass along faith from
    one generation to another
FAITH BIAS: one's own faith expression or the faith stance
    of a community of people

The intent of this book is to explore with other nurturers of adolescent
faith the importance of our calling, the direction of our ministry, and
the ingredients of the adolescent faith journey.

I want to begin confessionally.

Several years ago I participated in a deacons' meeting of my church in which these women and men were interviewing junior high candidates for baptism. The youth were asked to share their faith with the deacons as the last requirement before baptism and church membership.

My task was to introduce briefly each young person, and then the deacons were to "interview" them. The interviewing turned out to be a cross-examination. The young people became pale with fear. I heard them use religious phrases of which they could not possibly know the meaning. I watched the deacons as they nervously "corrected" the beliefs of the young people. The chairperson had begun the meeting by stating that he wanted an honest and informal sharing of faith. Instead, each answer was evaluated with doctrinal scrutiny. I noticed that the youth spoke in such soft voices as barely to be heard. They rarely looked up. The deacons seemed uncertain in their task of interviewing. The youth were uncertain in their responses. I watched with equal uncertainty, knowing that something was wrong but not knowing what to do.

After the session was over, we recognized that we had not heard an honest account of the decisions the youth had made. We had heard what we wanted to hear. Despite all our good intentions, we had failed to communicate affirmation of the youth or of their faith.

I emerged from that experience with two observations: First, there is a problem with the way the church engages in the nurturing of faith with adolescents. And second, there is insecurity and insensitivity among adult nurturers relative to the genuine faith-needs of youth.

Several years and many failures and successes later, I still identify those concerns as the greatest arenas in which more attention needs to be devoted: *the faith development emphasis of the local church and a better understanding of the task of being an adult nurturer of faith.*

The Church's Problem with Adolescent Faith Nurturing

The church is sold a false bill of goods when it accepts the idea that the nurturing of faith in adolescents is accomplished through a shortsighted program that often neither nurtures youth nor inspires faith. Adolescent faith development is frequently walled off in an isolated corner of the church's priorities. Even among churches who truly care about youth, there is noticeably absent a broad-based consciousness about how to nurture faith.

Most churches use one or more of these misdirected approaches as their only faith development effort with youth:

The Aisle Approach

The altar call is the only way to respond to the faith needs of youth. Get a conversion decision out of them. Once they are saved, the important work is done. Let's get youth walking down the aisle.

The Batch Approach

A faith decision is embarrassing to young people when they are singled out. Our faith nurturing is accomplished by taking a batch of them at a time, having them sit with the pastor in a month-long class, and then baptizing them on Palm Sunday.

The Osmosis Approach

We don't do a conscious thing. We believe that by our example faith will rub off naturally. Faith is contagious, you know!

The Busybody Approach

Keep these kids busy! Fill their time with church activities. Don't give them a chance to examine other alternatives, and they'll be strong, active Christians.

The Rob-the-Cradle Approach

Get to them early. Child evangelism never hurt anybody. If you present the faith to them before they are old enough to have so many questions and doubts, they will accept it more easily.

The Institutional Approach

We stress church membership. Faith is too elusive for most young people to understand. They can relate to the tangible demands of church membership. Talk about belonging, and believing will eventually follow.

These approaches naively assume that faith development with youth is an activity exclusively related to baptism, confirmation, conversion, or church membership. There is an emphasis on a one-time decision of faith. The personal faith journey from childhood through adolescence and into the adult years is largely overlooked.

The far more difficult task is to determine how to nurture, day in and day out, a mature development of faith. The task is really the nurturing of a lifetime of faithfulness that takes its shape in adolescence but extends throughout the adult years.

These approaches represent the institutional problem which faith development must overcome. An equally demanding problem is the personal confusion and uncertainty among the adults engaged in faith nurturing in the church and the home.

The Personal Problem with Adolescent Faith Nurturing

Every religion has the concern of passing along the faith to younger generations. Yet for all of their concern, Christian adults and parents today seem ill-equipped—in a world of increasingly competitive values, philosophies, and life-styles—to know how to be helpful to youth as they shape their faith.

Speak honestly with adults inside and outside the church, and you will become bewildered by their display of uncertainty, confusion, anguish, and fear as they raise questions about their responsibility of faith nurturing:

—How strongly should I advocate my own faith position with youth?

—Do I "hand" faith to youth, or do they create their own?

—If I feel inadequate in my faith, do I have anything to share with young people?

—Isn't baptism or confirmation all that I should expect from youth?

—What kind of faith should I attempt to pass along?

—Shouldn't all lifelong faith commitments be postponed until the adult years?

—How do I overcome embarrasssment and reticence to discuss matters of faith?

—Is this the responsibility of the home? . . . of the church? . . . of the school?

—Can't faith nurture just wait until they're sixteen and then have a once-and-for-all discussion?

—Can I really teach faith? Isn't it caught rather than taught? Won't it just naturally rub off?

—Isn't there a simple, no-lose method to inspire faith?

—Haven't we, as a scientific and technological society, outgrown the dependency on faith?

—Is faith able to compete with all of the material and ego satisfactions available to youth today?

—Among all the responsibilities of a parent or adult model to youth, how important is the responsibility of faith development? How much effort need it require?

In our secular society many sincere adults doubt that the nurturing of the faith of young people is a necessary responsibility. Even Christian, churchgoing adults often feel inadequate, embarrassed, reluctant, unskilled, or uninterested in the process of how youth acquire faith. There are legitimate concerns and questions to be voiced:

Frank grew up in a strict fundamentalist home. His father was a preacher who, in Frank's words today, felt the church was more important than his family. Much of his father's energy was invested in the church. All family members were thoroughly immersed in the faith. Now, with the children in their twenties, none of them expresses the slightest interest in church or matters of faith. Frank is reluctant to show any interest for fear of getting swallowed up. *Can the busyness and preoccupation of adult faith cause rejection in youth?*

Calvary Church is in turmoil with its youth ministry. Some adults and some of the high school youth think that the ministry has been too recreational in nature. They want more serious content and a more intentionally Christian format used in programming. The opposing group, which also includes some youth, feels that one must meet youth "where they are." They think church must be fun and enjoyable for youth. They fear that without the recreational thrust the enticement will slip away. A third group, though smaller, feels that the youth should not be separated in any way from the rest of the church. Their opinion is that by thorough participation in the total life of the church, youth truly learn what the church and Christian faith involve. The church's youth ministry has nearly come to a standstill because of the disagreements. *Does unanimity or consensus in faith nurturing in the church guarantee faith development?*

Joe has just graduated from high school. His family attends church every week and is quite active. His mother is very expressive in her faith. The father, quiet and steady, participates in his own ways. The church has a vibrant ministry with youth. Yet the son was turned off to the church during his last year in high school and now has completely dropped out. *Can all the good efforts and intentions still result in failure? Does anything "work"?*

Larry and Sarah are highly educated teachers. They are professional in nearly everything they attempt. They are liberal, free-thinking, active members of their church. For them, the cultural, academic, and recreational pursuits of their teenage children are as important, if not more so, than spiritual matters. They have high expectations of their children in all other matters, but in faith development they want their children to take their own steps. *Must faith development be a high priority?*

Daryl and Nancy are parents of young children. They are active for the first time in a church. Their involvement has been thoughtful and purposeful. Yet they feel woefully inadequate, insecure, and embarrassed about developing an atmosphere of faith nurturance in their home. They feel frightened to discuss it with someone who could be of help, because it sounds too stupid and obvious to bring up. *Why is faith such a difficult subject to discuss?*

Jack was an active participant in the church. When he reached senior high, he found himself the center of attention by his pastor, his youth group sponsors, his parents, and his church school teachers. They were all concerned that Jack had not yet made the decision to be baptized. The pastor finally was able to penetrate Jack's hesitancy and helped Jack make an honest confession of faith. Soon after, he was baptized. Six months later, Jack feels forgotten by all of these concerned adults. He still has questions, but no one seems willing to take the time to follow through with him. He wonders if faith is just a one-time decision to make and then to forget. *Is faith a lifelong journey or a one-time decision?*

Sarah just graduated from high school. Her church has no ministry with young adults because most of them leave town or are uninterested. Her parents are in the class and fellowship group nearest to her post-high-school age. She feels unwanted by the church.

Is peer group ministry an inherent part of faith shaping?

Linda is a teenager who is extremely loyal to her church. She is a committed Christian. Her parents are completely apathetic toward the church and will do nothing to encourage her involvement. They often plan conflicting family events, seemingly to interfere with Linda's church commitments. Until Linda was thirteen, she had no contact with the church and in her home there has never been any obvious traditions of spiritual nurturing. *Why do some youth express faith in spite of insurmountable odds?*

Many other examples could be cited to point out the complexities and murkiness with which most people approach the nurturing of faith with adolescents. From this confusion four hypotheses can be drawn:

1. Many adults place little value or energy in faith nurturing of youth. To them, it is given a low priority. It gets crowded to the edges by other concerns.

2. Many adults seem embarrassed or insecure when faith nurturing of youth is discussed.

3. Many adults are authoritarian and/or exploitive with their faith by thrusting it upon children and youth. Sometimes this is to cover up their own faith anxieties.

4. Many adults do not understand how faith is developed within youth and thus miss many positive opportunities to nurture faith. Few adults receive any training or guidance in this area.

The level of confusion regarding faith nurturing is rampant not only among the laity, but also even pastors and other professional leaders working with youth in the church can often be identified by one of these three divergent approaches:

1. *The "liberal"* is reluctant to be direct about matters of faith for fear of being manipulative or exploitive, will build ministries of outreach and group relationship, but do only subtle religious nurturing.

2. *The "pusher"* will sell and hawk the faith at every opportunity, often will allow the end of salvation to justify every means, will use powers of persuasion to help youth make faith decisions.

3. *The "nurturer"* realizes that youth have to make their own faith decisions but that they also need to be surrounded by a warm, positive environment that encourages spiritual expression and growth, recognizes that youth need honest assistance in shaping their own faith.

Obviously, I prefer the nurturing influence. It is my prayer that we inspire more lay and professional leaders, parent and adult models, to become nurturers.

Society's Contexts No Longer Reinforce

Because our society is increasingly pluralistic and our young people are exposed to a wide variety of options at increasingly younger ages, *we must acknowledge that this is a new era for faith nurturing*. No longer do the school, the church, the media, the neighborhood, the vocation, the social contacts, and popular culture reinforce one another. Today they offer competing ideas and philosophies. Chances are that the local disc jockey, the pastor, and the basketball coach are all influencing in opposing directions.

In a more homogenous day, a "total" environment for faith development was pervasive. Most social functions assumed a certain faith stance, and activities contributed to the faith nurturing of young people in some way.

In today's increasingly pluralistic churches, there is difficulty in providing a supportive environment for faith shaping. This leads to only one logical conclusion: *if faith nurturing is important, then we must create effective and intentional ways to accomplish it*.

Two institutions in particular must not be deceived. If the family thinks the church will teach its children all they need to know and thus expends no focused attention of faith development in the home, or if the church limits its role as a faith nurturer, both will be failing in a prime responsibility. The home as a primary family living together and the church as a family of faith serve as partners in this task. In American culture today, a strong supportive partnership between the church and home is the most effective design for mature faith nurturing of our youth and children.

The day has come for *an entirely new level of consciousness and intentionality regarding adolescent faith nurturing in the church and home*. Underneath, if not on the surface, young persons are pleading for help in facing life's ultimate, and therefore most important, questions. If faith is life's foundation, then we had best help youth to build it before we worry a great deal with the appearance of the structure. "The greater the building that has to be erected, the greater the need that the foundation be good. Religion is the most inclusive and most far-reaching aspect of life, and requires adequate foundations.''[1]

No One Escapes Faith!

There is in every human life an innate need to shape a personal faith. The need for faith is lifelong, though for most people the need is decidedly more intense and has a qualitatively different pace during adolescence. The emphasis during adolescence is on shaping faith. Most adolescents need to give tentative shape and form to a belief in the Ultimate. The beginning foundations laid during the teen years are sometimes outgrown, but they do have a lifelong effect. The term "faith shaping" refers to the intensity during the adolescent years of giving one's own faith a distinctive form.

The universal faith questions are these: "What is it that makes my life ultimately meaningful and satisfying? What is it that makes my life complete and whole?" The question of faith at any age can be phrased: "Where do I place my ultimate trust? When all else fails, what do I believe in?" The object of one's faith is one's "god."

In truth, many of us are polytheists. We create a variety of idols in various gradations, and our esteem and loyalty to them varies with maturation and even mood. But our *ultimate* trust or faith is more like a bedrock, and most people build their lives upon some faith foundation.

The tiniest infant places ultimate trust or faith in whatever is the source of food and relief. As time goes by, a young child transfers ultimate trust to parents. Through one's experiences and maturation, the deeper and more profound becomes one's faith. Many adults, however, do not answer the questions of faith at any deeper level than many children. Yet it is common to find high school youth grappling with sophisticated faith questions and creating for themselves a very mature faith stance.

It is common for children to express some response to the church or to God. Indeed, it is uncommon for them not to make some response. In some traditions, children, ages seven through twelve, make a decision of discipleship. That is the extreme, but it does give evidence that religious stirrings occur throughout childhood, adolescence, and the adult years.

During adolescence, however, most people first come to grips with

[1]R. S. Lee, *Your Growing Child and Religion* (New York: Macmillan, Inc., 1963), p. 15.

the limitedness of their own resources. They begin to investigate seriously the resources beyond themselves. Even though every teenager or young adult engages in this process of giving shape to personal faith, we know so very little about how to encourage it, direct it, or stimulate it.

The Question of Faith Quality

The basic question is, *"What quality of faith will our youth have?"* Will it be a faith that is satisfying in the ultimate sense? Will it be a faith that nourishes and induces personal growth? Could this faith provide helpful resources beyond what they would possess without it? Will this faith cause them to be more open and less defensive? . . . more able to interpret life's experience? . . . more able to act upon life? . . . more able to realize their potential? There are the questions of faith that apply to every teenager's life.

We can identify two concerns at this point:

1. How can adults pass along their faith in a mature and helpful manner to youth?

2. How can adults continue to grow in such a way as to pass along a truly mature and helpful faith to youth?

The first question has to do with the faith nurturing of youth and the second with the faith nurturing of adults. The questions are absolutely interrelated.

I would suggest that an important part of any thinking about how youth acquire faith must consider the quality of the faith we want youth to acquire and the quality of the faith adults are unconsciously modeling for youth.

Obviously no one's faith is perfect, but some models of faith are more positive than others. In a later chapter in this book (chapter 9) I will describe one theological model that does, in my opinion, respond to the questions listed above.

One of the difficulties in faith nurturing of youth is how confused so many churchs are as to their own convictions. In many churches the pastor or leadership dictates public belief. But even in those churches, people still have their own private belief. Too often externally enforced faith is a facade covering up the real thing.

In churches that stress individual freedom of belief, a laissez-faire attitude frequently exists without standards or criteria for belief. My congregation has just completed writing, for the first time in its 154-year history, a church covenant. It is not a creed, but a promise, a stating of the claims of our relationship with God. The covenant has given the church a healthy sense of pride, as well it should. It attempts to provide a positive, active model of faith to undergird not only our faith nurturing of youth but also the entire ministry of our church. Such a model is needed in many churches today, as a reminder, if nothing else, of their faith. The church (and the home) must offer a faith worth believing, a faith worth living.

They Deserve Our Bias

Let us question for a moment an assumption made throughout this book. The assumption is: *"We have the right to influence our children and youth with our own values, prejudices, and faith. There is no such thing as a pure environment in which youth can choose on their own what is important for them. Inculturation and socialization of the young are not exploitive acts."*

To negate this assumption reflects a naiveté about the purpose of childrearing.

Life is biased! The moment we speak one language to a child, life is biased. When we choose to accept one value rather than another, life is biased.

The bias is what makes life human. Upon thorough reflection, who would want our world to be any other way? Indeed, most good things about our lives are derived from the richness of family and cultural bias and heritage.

The bias is what makes life profound, rich, and meaningful. Humankind is forever in search of meanings, rituals, symbols, and ideals—faith! Every parent, civilization, church, and environment nurtures a faith bias in subtle, unconscious ways throughout the life of the young person.

That is not to say that every bias we have is good or healthy. Prejudice is a bias and an obviously distorted one. We constantly need to be shaping our bias (our mind-set) in more mature ways. Martin Luther King, Jr., once said,

> Softmindedness is one of the basic causes of race prejudice. The tough minded person always examines the facts before he reaches conclusions; in short, he postjudges. The tenderminded person reaches a conclusion

before he has examined the first fact; in short, he prejudges and is prejudiced.[2]

The point to be made is that while not every bias is mature, we still must recognize that all of human life is biased. There is no option to be impartial or unbiased in the way you live your life.

It is strange, therefore, that there is a contemporary mood of caution about inculcating our values upon our children and youth. Some of this has to do with the pluralistic age in which we live, some with the uncertainties that adults have of the values they hold, and some with an emphasis on the young person being free to select his or her own values, as opposed to the adult providing the values.

It is naive to believe that the important persons in a teenager's life should never advocate their own values. That is to be as silly as to say that one value is as good as another and it really doesn't matter which you prize. In some societies, the eating of human flesh is valued. In other societies, the worth of the individual is not valued. In some homes, jealousy is valued. To say that these are values as worthy in quality as the values of concern for persons, as forgiveness of others' wrongs, as sensitivity to feelings, is to open oneself to be regarded as a fool! One value is *not* as good as another. A thoughtful person would never say that it doesn't matter what you believe just as long as you believe something!

There is nothing worse than to damn our children by attempting to rear them in a sterile environment where no beliefs are cherished, no faith is upheld, no ideals followed, and no god esteemed. Such an upbringing is literally unhuman and inhuman. Adults who camouflage their faith, who are reluctant or cautious to share their faith bias freely, openly, and continuously, are subjecting their children to a cruel injustice. To do so is a form of spiritual child abuse that results in long-term detriment.

One of my fears is that Western society is slowly gravitating toward a licentious style of childrearing. Our goal is really to grant our young people freedom. But freedom and license are two different things. Freedom is gained by standing within a certain set of commitments. License comes with the attempt to live with no responsibilities

---

[2] Taken from a sermon, "A Tough Mind and a Tender Heart," in Martin Luther King, Jr., *Strength to Love* (New York: Harper & Row, Publishers, Inc., 1963), p. 4.

and no convictions. License is the ability to do whatever I want, whenever I want, to whomever I want. License is a selfish, hedonistic view that looks out only for one's own self. Such a position is a far distance from the other-centered stance of Jesus of Galilee.

I have met one person who forthrightly verbalized a philosophy of intending to raise her children in an unbiased faith orientation. The person had a doctorate in childhood education and was a leading educator. She had decided that faith was only an adult affair and that she would not influence her children one way or another. When she determined her children had reached a certain level of maturity, she would for the first time introduce ideas of faith.

Perhaps this mother represents the so-called "modern" parent who does not want to restrict or distort a child's world by rooting him or her in any faithful understanding of one's life or of the world in which he or she lives.

But those in this "modern" perspective are really kidding themselves if they think they are rearing their children in an unbiased home. Faith is much too pervasive. It cannot be "left out" of the human environment.

When I was in this mother's home, she had consciously "left out" a Christian perspective in her childrearing. But it did not take long to realize that instead of a Christian faith, the unconscious faith being modeled in that home was one that prized cold, academic intellectualism. It supported an abstract, detached, scientific world view and abhorred traditional public religious commitment. And this educator's children were deeply steeped in that faith bias.

Faith Nurturing Does Require Conscious Effort

If, from the above example, we can surmise that children live with our faith bias daily and cannot escape this influence, then why does faith nurturing require any conscious effort? Why can't it just happen?

For several reasons, *effective faith nurturing does require thoughtful and continuous effort*. Although the outward manifestations of our faith bias might be obvious to our children, the inward motivation of our faith will not be so obvious. To communicate that motivation takes more effort. Faith is intimate, and we rarely learn the intimate part of a person's life unless it is consciously shared. Faith is foundational, and it must be lifted up in order to be seen and understood.

As in the example of the educator above, if we do not make our faith explicit, we often send confusing signals to our children and youth. Hardly anyone lives up to the faith one professes. Most of us are sporadic in our faithfulness. By living faith intentionally and consciously, we send a more effective message to youth.

And, finally, in faith nurturing we are concerned not only to share our faith bias as adults but also to help young persons develop their own faith stance, and that requires conscious effort.

For these three reasons (to share the inner motivations of our faith, to send clear signals that link intention and behavior, and to help the young persons as they shape their own faith) it is imperative that adults treat faith development as a conscious responsibility.

Positively Nurturing a Faith Bias

There are many ways to nurture positively an adult faith bias in youth that (1) communicates the richness of the adult's faith bias and (2) frees the young person as he or she personalizes his or her own faith.

There are times to model our faith and times to enable youth to discover what is unique to their own faith.

Youth today need to grow up in an environment that is
—in touch with their own heritage,
—rich in expression of family ritual and faith,
—steeped in authentic tradition,
—expressed by participation in a larger community of faith, and
—ultimately freeing so that as children mature into adolescents, they are allowed more and more to create something of their own choosing.

Young persons need to be exposed to a faith orientation throughout their childhood and adolescence, but need never to have it thrust upon them in dictated ways.

A delicate balance must be our goal in helping youth acquire faith. We need to surround children and youth, but not smother them, with our ideas of faithfulness. Pass the faith, but do not push it. Parents, teachers, pastors, adult models, and friends are not salespersons of the faith. Faith is too respected a thing to be placed on the auction and sold to the highest bidder. It is not to be sold but acted out, modeled, prized, offered, and recommended. To meet in the "back-rooms" of our homes and churches plotting tactics to "con" our young people into belief is an incredible wrong.

Faith naturally has a compelling quality when it is allowed to grow and mature. I am always drawn to a faith that is growing and deepening, even when I might not agree with the content of the faith.

Is Faith Nurturing of Children and Youth Important?

Not only is faith nurturing important, but also once basic nutritional and health needs have been met, there is little that is more important! The faith bias is what gives each person a unique orientation to life. It is the only ingredient that enables us to interpret life's experiences or to place values on experience.

John Westerhoff wrote an important book which was titled with a probing question: *Will Our Children Have Faith?* [3] I would doubt that there is anything more important in God's eyes than how we answer that question. We can rightfully paraphrase Jesus' statement to say, "What good does it do a child if we provide clothes, housing, and school and do not properly ground her or him in faith?" or, "What good will it do us parents or adults if, in trying to save the world, we fail to share with our child what it is that gives our lives the deepest sense of meaning and fulfillment?" We must remember that there is no group of persons on whom a church can have more impact than it can have upon its children and youth. There is no group of persons on whom a home can have more impact than the young persons in that home.

At one point Jesus' disciples were caught up in competition, attempting to assert their own power over one another. As they walked to Capernaum, they were trying to decide who was first among them. When they arrived at their destination, Jesus pulled them aside and said, "Whoever is first among you must place himself last!" And then he took a child who happened to be nearby, and Jesus asked him to stand in front of the disciples. Jesus put his arms around the child and said to the disciples, "Whoever welcomes in my name one of these children, welcomes me; and whoever welcomes me, welcomes not only me but also the one who sent me" (Mark 9:36-37, TEV).

That symbolism is strong and direct! *It highlights the task of the*

[3] John H. Westerhoff III, *Will Our Children Have Faith?* (New York: A Crossroad Book, imprint of The Seabury Press, Inc., 1976).

adult to welcome children and youth into the loving reality of God's kingdom on earth. It is not our task to push or to force or to avoid. Our task is to welcome. Whoever opens the door in the name of Jesus to one of these children opens the door to the Lord God. What stronger mandate for faith nurturing do we need?

We owe it to our children and youth to share with them our faith bias!

Chapter 2

The Act of Welcoming

Faith advocacy . . . and faith clarification are important roles. Without resourceful adults willing to stand in these roles, our efforts in welcoming youth into the faith will lack integrity and effectiveness.

FAITH CLARIFICATION: a behavior in which an attempt is made to help a young person clarify his or her faith questions

FAITH ADVOCACY: a behavior in which an attempt is made to bring the faith nearly or directly to the young person

NEARNESS: bringing faithful activities and traditions near to youth; making them an integral part of their upbringing

DIRECTNESS: bringing the faith directly to young persons; presenting the claims of the faith in an open-ended and appealing way

The adult responsibility in helping youth acquire faith is to welcome them into faith! This simple statement sets forth a challenging agenda.

For what is implied by welcoming is both (1) standing by the "door of faith" to greet and make a place for youth as they enter and (2) presenting faith and its traditions as a welcome and desirable ingredient of daily life. To welcome into faith is thus not a one-time event, nor is it only a program of the local church. It is the consistent provision by adults of a total context for growth throughout the days of childhood and adolescence.

In this chapter we shall explore specific adult behaviors that are helpful to youth as they shape their faith. In the next chapter we will discuss the need and scope of memorable faith experiences.

Faith Clarification and Faith Advocacy

Two behaviors describe how adults can best guide adolescent faith development: Faith Clarification and Faith Advocacy. Adults need to learn effective, noncoercive ways to advocate faith and to clarify faith.

To advocate is to share our faith bias by bringing it nearly and directly to young persons. To advocate is never to decide for the young person but, rather, to be positive and wholesome supporters of faith. Clarifiers do not advocate faith to youth. Instead they stand in a readily available yet neutral stance.

How Do We Clarify Faith with Youth?

Faith clarification is a behavior which adults can practice that helps a young person in the process of faith shaping. Rather than provide answers, the faith clarifier raises questions that might point the young person toward his or her own answers.

The faith clarifier is a person who opens up choices for the young person. The clarifier lifts up a moral dilemma, a theological question, or a provocative idea that the young person has shared so that it may be freely discussed and alternative ideas considered. When the young person reaches a decision, that decision is respected, though it may not be one with which the adult agrees.

In faith clarification the intent is not for adults to share their own faith bias with young people. Faith clarification is the process of helping young people. Faith clarification is the process of helping young people focus upon the growing edge of their own faith. It includes *being sensitive* to areas of confusion where growth is needed, *helping youth identify* the problem and explore alternatives, and *being a resource* to the youth as they are involved in the task of shaping their own faith.

Faith clarification is quite similar to values clarification. Actually, our faith is a set of beliefs and convictions that we most value or prize. When we clarify faith, we clarify those values in which we most trust and upon which we most deeply depend. Unfortunately, some advocates of values clarification uphold this approach to the exclusion of all other nurturing behaviors. They feel that healthy adults will clarify values with youth but never advocate values with youth. But there is need to do both. The fact is that we cannot help advocating values because, as we have noted earlier, life is biased. When we live out a conviction in everyday life before our children, we are advocates. What we need to do is develop skills and plans to advocate in healthy ways, to avoid manipulation, and to evaluate our behavior to make it consistent with those values we most want to claim.

The Clarifier and Advocate as One

Young persons need adult advocates and clarifiers. In the advocacy role we are emphasizing commitments, in clarification choices. If youth know that an adult is capable and willing to act in both capacities, they will find ways to let the adult know which they are seeking. The task of the adult is to learn to be sensitive to what youth are seeking and not to operate by his or her own assumptions.

Indeed, the clarifying and advocating behaviors are also important for adults to experience as well as youth. When I push against the growing edge of my faith out to the "frontiers" of my convictions, I look to other respected persons of faith sometimes for advocacy ("This is the way of faith") and sometimes for clarification ("What makes you believe that this is the way of faith?"). All Christian journeyers need advocates and clarifiers.

Some parents who have been actively involved with faith development during their children's younger years might be seen by their teenagers as such strong advocates of faith that the role of clarifier might be more difficult to see. If this is true, then it only points toward the need for the church to be a place where adults, other than parents, are encouraged and empowered to build significant relationships with youth. Another adult can sometimes fulfill the role of clarifier with ease when that would be nearly impossible for a parent and vice versa.

Young people are doubly blessed when the same person can be

both a faith clarifier and a faith advocate. If a person has strong convictions but does not force them upon another nor insist upon agreement with them, if that person not only allows but encourages thoughtful questions, that person truly models the role of clarifier and advocate.

How Do We Advocate Our Faith to Youth?

There are two ways to advocate our faith to youth: by *nearness* and by *directness*.

Nearness

How "near" are faithful activities to youth? If faithful traditions rarely enter the home, then they are not near. If the stories of the faith are heard only through occasional or casual church attendance and nothing more, then faith is even further removed from that young person. There must be a nearness (closeness) to the faithful community and its traditions, rituals, and stories. *Being near to the faith is pivotal for youth.*

The faith is near when Christian adults live their faith in natural ways before the young person. The faith is near when the young person feels that he or she is a close part of the church. The faith is near when the young person is allowed deep relationships with adult Christian models. The faith is near when families are not embarrassed to express faith and when parents are public with their commitments. The faith is near when families develop and practice faithful traditions in the home with regularity. The faith is near when youth can see how much faith is prized by the important adults around them. The home and the church must be in harmony on the importance of faith.

Nothing brings the faith nearer than the way in which the parents prize their own faith and their own relationship with the church. If faith is of great importance, then the child will be brought near to it. If it is not, the chances are the child will feel more distant from it.

Many churches and homes get started on the wrong foot by delaying patterns of nearness for their young children. But it is rarely too late to reverse habits. Parents and churches who change their priorities midstream and allow new priorities to have an impact can often be successful in imparting faith to children. One set of parents claimed personal belief themselves but were lax in sharing this with their children. They communicated a casualness regarding faith to their children which they really did not intend. Finally, the arrest of their oldest son caused them to establish new priorities for their lives. They made a new commitment to bring the faith nearer to their children. They carefully changed their parental styles and grew to become outstanding models who had a significant and life-changing impact on bringing their faith traditions near to their children in the home and through the church.

Many parents are deceived about how near they bring the faith to youth. The assertions "I took my child to church every Sunday," "I served on a committee down there for a while," or "We prayed before every meal in our home" are indicative of the misunderstanding. When these things are done out of compulsion or obligation, or when they are done perfunctorily, or when they are done with little personal investment, the nearness of faith does not truly exist.

Some churches plan activities and groups for youth, but youth do not genuinely feel prized or included in the church fellowship. Nearness will not be encouraged. Other churches plan activities and groups for youth that rarely focus upon faith development. The events are designed merely to keep youth busy and occupied. Nearness will not be encouraged. Still other churches plan activities and groups that approach faith in a staid, unrelated way. They speak of faith only in terms of clichés. Nearness, again, will not be encouraged.

The New Testament speaks mainly of first-generation adult Christians; so it is difficult to cite an example of nearness from its pages. Paul, however, in his second letter to Timothy, does speak of nearness in Timothy's upbringing. Timothy was as close to Paul as a son would be to a father. Paul speaks of him in 2 Timothy 1:2-3 as "my beloved child . . . whom . . . I remember constantly in my prayers." Paul was an important role model for this young man. In 2 Timothy 1:5, Paul says, "I am reminded of your sincere faith, a faith that dwelt first in your grandmother Lois and your mother Eunice and now, I am sure, dwells in you."

It is clear that Timothy is a third-generation Christian and owes much of his faithfulness to his grandmother and mother. It is also clear that Timothy has been raised as a youth near to the church, near to its faithful traditions, near to a home where faith was prized and enjoyed, near to important adult Christian models, near to a whole community of friends who did not fear to speak of their commitments, even in the face of adversity.

Paul uses this reminder of the nearness of faith in Timothy's younger years to encourage him to persevere, to take his share of suffering. Paul says it is the nearness that will be an anchor to him.

A young person who is strongly influenced by the nearness of the faith is one who more than likely experiences a gradual, undramatic conversion, as is suggested by Timothy's upbringing.

Directness

Plainly stated, there must be specific times when the faith is presented directly to the young person. In some churches, we "beat around the bush" too much. We're often embarrassed in our homes to bring up concerns of faith. We feel insecure because we might not be able to answer all questions with precision. Often main-line church families are so cautious not to coerce or manipulate that they err on the side of neglect.

Directness is the presenting of Christian faith claims to a young person in an appealing, fair, and open-ended way. Directness is not to suggest a simplistic "salvation pitch" which is given until the young person finally relents. That is gross manipulation more in the interest of the adult than of the youth. Youth have enough external pressures upon them; we need not make of religion yet another.

The directness we use in presenting faith needs to happen in relation to a teenager's maturity and development. It needs to happen on God's timetable and not on ours. It also needs to happen in different settings and at different points along the way.

Directness occurs when we intentionally aid young persons in writing a new chapter in their faith story. Directness means frank questions and discussions with youth about the meaning of personal faith. Directness includes occasions when worship is intimate, when prayer touches, when service is eye-opening. Directness happens when we intentionally (though it may be spontaneous) help youth address their own questions of faith. Directness occurs when we share our own faith story and faith bias. Directness is different from faith clarification in that adults are directly bringing their own faith to young persons in an advocacy role.

A young person who tends to be more influenced by the directness in which the faith is presented is one who more likely experiences a specific, eventful conversion. The most famous New Testament example is the conversion of the apostle Paul, who was known as Saul before his sudden new commitment. Saul, a persecutor of Christian faith, was on the road to Damascus when he was struck down. Several days later, he rose up again, a new person of faith. The faith was brought directly to him, in a one-time experience, and he accepted. (See Acts 9.)

Nearness and Directness Work Together

Nearness and directness are two avenues by which we can advocate our faith to youth. Their worth is enhanced when allowed to complement each other. Faith can be advocated *nearly* to a person from the moment of birth on, through the developmental stages. Faith is advocated *directly* to older children and adolescents in response to their inquiry and questioning. Faith should be brought directly with greater frequency in the teen years. With those youth who will not reach the stage of faith inquiry until their early adult years, directness may be offered earlier, but it will not be "heard." There is nothing wrong with this. People mature in different areas of their lives at different paces.

Let us cite examples of nearness and directness in the faith development of two young persons.

Janet was a young girl who first came to my church's youth group by way of a friend. She came from a family inactive in their own church. It wasn't long before Janet was a full participant in everything that we did. In fact, she became a leader among our youth. During one of our major musicals, she played the lead part. We developed in a short time quite a pattern of nearness with Janet. Janet and I had had short bits and pieces of talk about faith. She had serious doubts about whether God existed. She was quite open with her questions. One time coming back to the church from a weekend outing, we were sitting alone in the front of the church bus. As I drove down out of the mountains, Janet and I discussed openly and searchingly her own relationship with God and her acceptance of God's love. Nothing came from this conversation in terms of a life-changing decision, but it was definitely a time of directness. To my knowledge Janet still has not claimed the Christian faith. But that is not my responsibility. My responsibility was to bring the faith nearly and directly to her.

Jack was a young person who came from an extremely thoughtful and faithful family. Both of his parents were articulate Christians. They had held nearly every office in the church. Both parents had been church school teachers on the adult and youth levels. They had a healthy marriage and good child-rearing practices. They were a model family of faith. Jack was their oldest child. He grew up as an active participant in his church and it was an important part of his life. The faith was brought directly and nearly to him both at home and at church. Halfway through his senior year, Jack needed distance between his own life and his upbringing. So he rebelled against the church. He was not hostile but just uninterested. There was no apparent reason or cause for the split, which ten months later was overcome. Throughout this separation his church and his parents expressed loving concern—but no coercion. Jack is moving back into the fellowship of his church, and he is still attempting to cultivate his own faith stance. Our responsibility was to bring the faith near to him and directly to him and allow him the freedom to respond to it at his own pace.

Faith was advocated in both of these illustrations. Faith clarification was an equally important ingredient in each stage of development as well. Janet wanted a clarifier to help her sort through her questions about God's existence. She would not have trusted any advocate of faith who did not first help her as she clarified her own unfolding stance. When Jack separated from the faith, he needed a clarifier, not an advocate, to stay in relationship with him during his time of alienation.

Faith advocacy (its nearness and directness) and faith clarification are important roles. Without resourceful adults willing to stand in these roles, our efforts in welcoming youth into faith will lack integrity and effectiveness.

Chapter 3

Memorable Faith

The church that would establish faith shaping as the most serious ingredient of its ministry with youth must be dedicated to the goal of providing its youth the best environment for positive memorable experiences.

MEMORY: your own unique collection of life's experiences
MEMORIES: specific recollections of experiences in your life

One of the prime goals for faith development of children and youth is to have an impact upon their memory.

A memory is a primary difference among a child, an adolescent, and an adult. An adult has a richer memory from which to draw as he or she shares his or her life and makes decisions than has a young person and certainly a child. The mature understanding of one's own life memories is the beginning of wisdom.

The Role of Memory

A memory is our own unique collection of life's experiences. Our memory informs our personal identity. The difference between memories, from person to person, is a key reason for our uniqueness as individuals. Memory is the only handle we have to our roots. It is the awareness of our reservoir of memory that is the beginning of the faith journey. As we become aware of what is in that vast reservoir, we attempt to sort it out and to create something meaningful of it.

We will not be able to make mature decisions about ultimate meaning, transcendence, or religious affiliation until we attempt to harmonize our disjointed memories into an understandable memory. A younger child does not yet understand her or his own memory. The child has many disjointed memories that do not connect with one another. For example, a young child will touch a hot oven once or twice. But soon the child remembers (pulls together these separate memories) that a hot oven burns and causes discomfort. Most adolescents are actively involved in the task of making sense of their experience (of understanding their memory). Workers with youth need to help them create order from their experience. Often, junior-high-age young persons begin to pull together faith experiences and memories. They may remember a kindly second grade teacher, a Children's Sunday in the fourth grade, a song they love to sing at Easter, prayers at their family table, and discussions in the sixth grade about the death of their favorite uncle. These separate memories are mulled over in the minds of junior high youth until they are understood. These separate memories are synthesized perhaps into a new belief, or value, or are shaped into a deeper faith.

We cannot be memoryless. We cannot "forget" our lives, though we can certainly forget some of its experiences. We will unconsciously be committing our lives to memory as we go. Not every experience of life is remembered with equal force. Our brains not only have a great capacity for storing memories, but they also have a selective, or filtering, capability. What we remember from any given experience is largely based upon what we are open to or looking for in that moment. I have no memory at all of my very first date when I was in junior high. Apparently, nothing of any lasting impression happened. I do, however, remember distinctly my first date with my wife because we spent the entire evening in a gas station getting my car fixed! That did leave an impression!

Only the child can control what he or she remembers and its

relative significance to him or her. Faith experiences can be forced on youth, but in their memory all that will be retained is the unpleasantness, not the content or meaning of faith.

Early memories influence the way we approach later experiences. A poignant memory of a very bad first date at age thirteen will have some impact upon the fifth date at age fifteen. If we have only memories of dissatisfaction, insensitivity, and carelessness from the first year of life, then we will find it more difficult as teenagers to accept concern, love, and happiness. We are not doomed to live out the past, but neither can we entirely escape it.

As we age and mature, we advance intellectually, relationally, and emotionally. We use these skills to interpret our memories and place them in perspective. The shape of memory is not maturely focused until mid-adulthood. It is shaped by the kinds of experience we remember from our childhood, adolescence, and young adulthood. A memory is shaped by our values, beliefs, and faith.

Faith development must be particularly interested in the memories of youth and children. Consider for a moment the nature of the Christian faith itself. The Bible is a collection of memories and stories told and retold. It is the dialogue of God acting in the history of people.

Without the stories of Adam and Eve, of Abraham moving out, of Moses and the bondage in Egypt, of Jesus' birth, death, and resurrection, . . . of Francis of Assisi, Luther, Bonhoeffer, and King, we would have no faith. Memories of our heritage of faith play such an integral part in Christianity because it is a historical religion. In a similar way personal memories, shaped within each individual, play an integral role in faith development.

If young persons have no important memories of the faith, of the church, of an experience of God, of worship, or of spiritual feelings, they will find themselves in a faith vacuum as young adults.

Influencing the Contexts of Memory and Experience

We can have little impact on how children and youth remember or on what will leave the strongest impression; but we do influence the scope of their experience.

In any civilization it is the responsibility of the adults to provide the contexts for the experience of the children and youth as well as to provide gradual freedom to select their own experience.

Adults cannot dictate all experiences of children or shelter them in any artificial way. Yet in the broadest sense children live within the limits set by the adults around them. Within those limits, in healthy situations, there is granted the freedom for even the youngest of infants to choose and explore. *The prime task of the adult is to set creative limits by determining the contexts for the child's behavior.* Adults should determine that the sandbox is a far better context for a three-year-old to play in than the streets. And that social play with other three-year-olds is a better context than sitting passively in front of the television set. The older the child, the broader the limits. Establishing guidelines for dating, for bedtime, for friendships, for homework, and for church involvement all involve a determination of the best context for the child.

For older, mature adolescents, the limits to their experiencing will approach the same limits as those experienced by adults around them: (1) limits of choice and (2) limits set by larger societal conditions. This will occur as adolescents prove themselves capable of handling new responsibility.

From our Christian tradition we want our children and youth to have experienced (1) recognition as a valued and gifted person; (2) love in the active setting of the church and the home; (3) acceptance of themselves as they are; (4) traditions that point toward God and faith; and (5) trust in themselves, in other people, and in God's will. Solid memories related to these five areas should be our goal for all young persons.

The Memories Are for Keeps

The scriptural admonishment is to

> Train up a child in the way he should go,
> and when he is old he will not depart from it.
> —Proverbs 22:6

Not long ago, two very caring Christian parents spoke with me about their son, now a young adult, who expresses no interest in the institutional church or in the Christian faith journey. They were worried that they had done something terribly wrong in his upbringing to cause such uninterest and such denial of his church heritage. They had been parents who tended to influence choices over commitments with their son, but they were superb Christian models. There was no way that their son could have missed their witness. At this point they had not forced the issue with him. I encouraged them to stay in communication and dialogue, never pushing but never dropping their concern. They needed to play a clarifier role. I also tried to help them feel confident in the quality of the memories that this young man carried within him. Someday he will want to sort them out and grow in deeper understanding. If the channels are kept open, the parents could be available to him when the moment of readiness arrives.

As an adult, I am still coming to grips with my own faith memories. For example, when I was in the eighth grade, I worked for Jack, owner of a small store. Jack was a close friend of my family as well as an active church deacon and my Sunday school teacher. One day at the store, Jack was apparently cheated by a wholesale salesman. I remember that he charged into the back room that day raving and ranting in such a way as I had never seen or heard, at least from a Baptist deacon. You might think that this experience convinced me of the hypocrisy or inconsistency of Christian adults, but it had quite the opposite impact.

I was unconscious of this memory until, at the age of twenty-seven, I was writing a sermon. In my preparation I realized what this single memory meant to the shaping of my faith. I learned that day, unconsciously but deeply, that Christians could be real persons. They could get angry in the right place and time. I learned that even my Sunday school teacher could lose his cool and express hostile feelings and still not lose the faith. That recall was a strategic lesson as I was reminded of the important role that memories play in the shaping of faith.

No matter what shape a young person gives her or his faith and no matter how foreign that might seem to her or his tutors, a young person will never be able to ignore her or his roots or memories. They will be a part of that person wherever she or he goes. Because (1) we can influence the scope of young people's memories and (2) memories are relatively permanent, there are some critically important ramifications for faith development here. All that a church does should be with significance or not done at all! *Boring, mundane experiences are faith defeating!!* What we have always feared is true: a boring offering of the faith will defeat our ability to nurture faith within youth! Note that the criteria is significance, not flash or pomp; not showmanship or intellectualism. If an experience will be significant or profound, the church should plan for it.

With children and youth we need intentionally to provide *memorable experiences* (experiences that they will likely remember).

We should be celebrating the Christian seasons in our homes and in our churches with imagination, with tradition, and with significance. We should be creating devotional traditions in our homes and personal lives that really matter! We should plan for some large-scale church events beamed at children and youth. We should live out the faith intergenerationally with potency! We should intentionally encourage strong adult models and create long-lasting relationships between adults and youth in the church, not only between advisers and youth.

Church school classes that create a life-size replica of the ark of the covenant provide far more potent memories than will those who sit in the classroom describing it for three weeks. Churches that plan a truly personal celebration for adolescents at the time of their baptism will create a lasting impression.

Retreats, camps, trips, conventions, musical or dramatic productions, active mission undertakings, in-depth relationships, significant opportunities for participation in the local church—all are important because of the memorable experiences they make possible.

Expenditures of time and money and talent to create some headline experiences can be defended, particularly for youth. The quality of the memory and the depth of its impact are far more important than the quantity. And this kind of experience does not require a large or sophisticated church. Size and quality are quite unrelated.

The significant experiences need not and should not only be geared to a single age level audience. Personal memories of intergenerational events and relationships are very important. The dedication of a new church building, the participation in a community service project, the washing of Communion cups with one's family each Sunday for months or years—all these can be instructive.

An Inventory of Memorable Experiences

As I think of what I have heard my wife express about the treasured faith memories of her upbringing, I recall these things:

1. the huge youth ministry with a youth-written weekly newspaper that she witnessed as a young child;

2. the annual Palm Sunday service that featured a joyous celebration of and for children;
3. her helping a relative clean up after Communion each month;
4. the faithfulness of her mother in transporting black inner-city children to and from the church;
5. the several adults who took an over-and-above interest in her life;
6. her being employed as an eighteen-year-old Neighborhood Staff member in her church's inner-city recreational program;
7. her own baptism at the same time as her sister's, soon to be followed by her father's baptism;
8. her being in a post-high-school group in which each member was asked to write a one-page statement of faith, which forced her to ask many first-time faith questions; and
9. a youth pastor of her church who faithfully transported her and her sister every weekend for two months to a distant hospital where her father was dying.

Some of her experiences were of the headline variety; some were done with enough repetition to make an impression; some were personally touching incidents, and some were significant relationships.

I would suggest the following as the Inventory of Faith Shaping Experiences which adults should facilitate with youth:

1. *"Headline" Experiences:* highlighted events; occurrences that are noteworthy (they usually require self-discipline and effort from the youth and concerted planning and support from adults). My wife being employed to do an inner-city ministry by her church was a headline experience for her.

2. *Repetitious Experiences:* those which stand in our tradition; things done with regularity (annually, weekly, daily, seasonally); our ritual. My wife's participation in Palm Sunday celebrations in her church was a repetitious experience. They did the same things and sang the same songs every year.

3. *Personally Touching Events:* feeling-oriented experiences; times when we are deeply affected; times when we are allowed and encouraged to be sensitively in touch. My father-in-law's baptism was a personally touching event for my wife, as was the presentation of her statement of faith to a support group as a young adult.

4. *Significant Relationships:* persons who are of prime importance to us; persons who support and trust us. The youth pastor who transported my wife when her father was dying stimulated a memory of a significant relationship.

Every church, no matter what the size or wealth, can provide a profound inventory of memorable experiences in each of these four categories. Each experience describes patterns of Nearness. Some could also apply to Directness. (See chapter 2.)

Sometimes we will plan specific events that we hope will be memorable for youth, but more precisely we are seeking to create *an environment or atmosphere in which healthy faith shaping can occur.*

Such an environment is not one where adult-youth relationships are merely planned but, rather, one where they are encouraged.

Such an environment is not one where sensitivity is carefully structured, but one where persons are encouraged to touch and be touched with their feelings.

In such an environment repetition is not laboriously followed but, rather, is the chosen and desired level of faithfulness.

In such an environment headline experiences are not ends in themselves but are means to a larger goal of faith shaping.

If you could stand in the shoes of your youth for a moment, could you evaluate your church and your family in each area of this inventory?

One difficulty in evaluating progress with adolescents is knowing what will be the long-term impact of these early, shaping experiences. Adolescent faith development is often tentative and unconscious. My wife, for example, resented as a child the intrusion of the inner-city black children her mother transported. It was only later in her life that this singular witness became a real model and inspiration for her. Effectiveness with youth (what really makes a positive impact in their lives) is difficult to evaluate in the short term.

The church that would establish faith shaping as the most serious ingredient of its ministry with youth must be dedicated to the goal of providing its youth the best environment for positive memorable experiences.

Chapter 4

Faith Shaping: How Youth Acquire Faith

Faith shaping is the task of acquiring one's own faith.

AFFILIATING: a child's attempt to identify and stand within the values and faith of the important persons in his or her life

PERSONALIZING: a young person's attempt to claim ownership of his or her own faith, in relation to the faith that has surrounded him or her in the formative years

INTEGRATING: an adult's attempt to build the faith she or he has recently personalized upon the faith inherited as a child

FAITH SHAPING: refers particularly to a process during adolescence and young adulthood when most persons actively give shape and substance to their own personal faith; the process of determining one's own faith

FAITH-SHAPING TASKS: a sequence of tasks through which young persons work as they acquire a personal faith

EXPERIENCING: spiritual emotions, religious feelings, sacred experiences

CATEGORIZING: sorting out and consolidating one's religious experiences; making sense of the experiences in understandable terms

CHOOSING: deciding what is true and important

CLAIMING: the act of commitment; conversion; giving one's life to something

DEEPENING: the act of maturing in one's faith commitments

SEPARATING: pulling away from earlier convictions and decisions; giving oneself space for reflection and consolidation; rebellion

RESPONDING: gaining a sense of one's life calling; discovering your own giftedness

READINESS: the next level of growth or maturity to which a person is receptive

This chapter focuses upon the heart of this book's concern: the sequence and tasks of growth as youth acquire personal faith. Three postures from which to view the patterns of growth will be considered.

First, we will take the posture of a developmental overview of faith. We will sketch the stages of faith as they unfold in the child, the adolescent, and the adult. This posture is the typical developmental one and will undoubtedly parallel those of other contributors [Wayne R. Rood, *On Nurturing Christians* (Nashville: Abingdon Press, 1972); John H. Westerhoff III, *Will Our Children Have Faith?* (New York: A Crossroad Book, imprint of The Seabury Press, Inc., 1976); James Fowler and Sam Keen, *Life Maps: Conversations on the Journey of Faith* (Needham Heights, Mass.: Wexford Press, 1977); John J. Gleason, Jr., *Growing Up to God: Eight Steps in Religious Development* (Nashville: Abingdon Press, 1975)]. Since these have offered significant insights into this perspective, we will sketch this approach briefly to "set the scene" for the second posture. We will, in the first posture, particularly, note those stages leading into adolescence from late childhood, and those leading from adolescence into young adulthood.

The second posture focuses upon the adolescent years to describe the specific tasks through which young persons work as they actively give shape and substance to their own personal faith. These tasks form the agenda for adolescents as they pass into this stage of faith maturity. This second posture describes the choices, experiences, decisions, needs, and ambiguities which they face.

The third and final posture will be a glance beneath the stages and tasks of faith development to that which motivates growth and to that which is the matrix for human maturing: individual readiness.

The First Posture: Stages of Faith Development

In this first posture, we will look at the stages of faith development, from childhood through adolescence into young adulthood. A chart at the end of this section will show the relationship of these stages to one another.

Affiliating with Faith

As children mature, most will want to affiliate themselves with the faith tradition that has been practiced and prized in their home and church.

Affiliating is a normal part of a childhood. Some persons never wish to affiliate with the church, even when their parents are active in it. There can be a variety of reasons for this. Some of the most common are a feeling of unpleasantness associated with the church, rigid parental attitudes toward religion, or a lax, apathetic attitude toward religious nurture.

Affiliating can be symbolized by the child through confirmation or believer's baptism, or it can simply be a feeling of the child upon which no formal action is taken. It can begin early in childhood or late in adolescence. And affiliating occurs in families whether or not they participate in a church. Parents exhibit faith and values. Children tend to identify with these.

Affiliating is a child's attempt to identify and stand within the values and faith of the important persons in his or her life. There is a developmental tendency within children to affiliate.

A depressed man recently came to my office for counseling. He had been living with a woman and her two sons for the past year. He had a deep love and respect for the boys. From his perspective the woman was a very inadequate mother who could not cope with her sons. It largely fell to him to dress and feed the boys, to teach and

nurture them. He did this with enthusiasm. The relationship he had with the boys was very special for the three of them. But as his relationship with the woman disintegrated, he was told to leave the home and never return. When he did return for a visit with the two boys when the mother was away, the boys completely disowned him, shouted hateful things at him, and spat upon him.

The man was in tears as he told this sad tale. The experience illustrates the sense of belonging those boys had as they sided with their mother, no matter how unhealthy she happened to be. Children do affiliate with the attitudes, feelings, and faith of their parents.

Personalizing Faith

At some point, every child begins to personalize the faith of his or her parents. The child creates from this faith something of his or her own. With many persons this personalizing begins to happen in middle childhood, becomes more active in adolescence, and peaks in the young adult years. It is prominent throughout the teen years. For most personalizing is a gradual process. For some it is marked by alienation, hostility, rebellion, and sporadic growth. For others, it is calm, reasoned, and cautious. Personality, the surrounding environment, and parental style are the most determinative factors in how personalizing takes place. Two children of the same parents often experience the personalizing of faith in radically different ways.

Personalizing is the young person's attempt to claim ownership of his or her own faith in relation to the faith that has surrounded him or her in the formative years. There is a developmental tendency within adolescence to personalize.

Personalizing is an attempt to claim ownership.

Affiliating is an attempt to claim membership.

As surely as affiliating requires affirmation and acceptance from important others, so does personalizing. With most young persons, personalizing the faith becomes more distinctive the older the young person becomes, and the more removed the person is from parental authority. Personalizing requires a self-centeredness, because the adolescent is trying to determine what is uniquely her or his own. This is the reason why adolescents sometimes appear "wrapped up" in themselves.

At the height of the personalizing of faith, an older young person might measure her or his growth by how different or opposite it is from the faith traditions she or he affiliated with during childhood years.

Integrating Faith

The surest sign of maturity for a young or middle adult is when she or he measures her or his personal growth *not by how different it is* from the faith she or he inherited from her or his parents, but by *how well her or his growth builds upon the foundations* laid during childhood years. The pendulum has begun to swing back into a more mature perspective.

Integration is the adult's attempt to build the faith she or he has recently personalized upon the faith inherited as a child. There is a developmental tendency in the adult years to integrate. Integration is the ability to take the good things from one's past and mold them together into a solid foundation for the facing of the future.

Bill was a young father, getting established in his career, buying a first home. He had grown up in the South in a fundamentalistic religious background. As a child and as an adolescent he was deeply immersed in inherited faith. When he went off to college, he rejected his faith heritage. He had no further contact with the church for years. During these intervening years, he largely avoided questions of faith.

Ten years later, Bill was still rebelling against his earlier memories of faith. However, no longer could he avoid asking questions of his own faith. There was now an emptiness that needed to be filled.

Bill mistakenly assumed that every church shared the same characteristics of the church he attended in childhood. When Bill came to my congregation, he discovered an openness and diversity more attuned to his present mentality. He was so unprepared for this style that it forced him to face those faith questions he had set aside so long ago.

Now Bill is struggling to reconcile an inherited faith that he sees as uncompromising with a personalized faith that he does not want to compromise. His personalized faith has taken the form of what he does *not* believe rather than a positive position. Bill is uncomfortable with one "foot" in both worlds. Yet he is worried that the chasm is too great to overcome. This young man is now entering the faith development stage of integrating. To mature fully, Bill must find ways to integrate the best from his affiliated faith with the best from his personalized faith.

The Broadest Developmental Picture

Let us attempt to stand back for a moment to examine the broadest developmental picture of faith. This chart shows a typical pattern but is not the only pattern of maturing.

TYPICAL PATTERN OF FAITH DEVELOPMENT

CHILDHOOD YEARS (preschool and primary school years)
- Times of discovering and then affiliating with the values, beliefs, and faith of parents (and church)

LATE CHILDHOOD AND EARLY TEEN YEARS (junior and junior high years)
- Living with the tension of taking the first step beyond a cultural or parental faith bias, accompanied by the most intense desire to affiliate with that bias
- A beginning of identity; of will; of asserting one's own person in the initial stages
- Often the young person formally affiliates with faith as "a personal decision" (confirmation/baptism)

MIDTEEN YEARS (high school years)
- An increase in tension between inherited and personalized faith
- Less parental faith influence; more influence accepted from other adults and peers
- Asserting individuality and identity; stepping beyond previous limits
- Often a time to be authentic to one's own chosen faith
- Interest in faith can vary from sporadic to latent to intense during these years

LATE TEEN YEARS AND EARLY TWENTIES (post–high school, college, early career)
- Often attempting to be very untraditional; experimentation with novel ideas of faith; restlessness

Years of Most Active Faith Shaping

Affiliation Years

Personalizing Years

(left margin, rotated) Years of Most Active Faith Shaping

(left margin, rotated) Personalizing Years

(left margin, rotated) Integrating Years

(left margin, rotated) Integrating Years

- Formulating the most important life directions amidst sporadic and hectic growth
- Rebelling against parental influence and separation from one's own heritage
- Coping with newfound adult independence; recognition of the inadequacy of one's own faith shaping

MIDTWENTIES TO MIDTHIRTIES (marriage, childbearing, establishing vocation)

- Formulating idealistic goals and dreams for life in midtwenties; refining of life goals to more realistic proportions by midthirties
- Integrating inherited faith with personalized faith (Having children and/or becoming a recognized contributor to society often hastens the integration; the question that new parents often ask is, "What is there from my past that I want and do not want my child to experience?")

THIRTIES TO SIXTIES

- Living out the reconciliation between personalized and inherited faith
- Gradual and stable maturation; periods of stagnation and periods of reexamination and change

SENIOR ADULT YEARS

- Broadened understanding and appreciation of life and faith; wisdom ascertained from life's experiences
- Ability to face death and life's consequences with more certainty and less fear
- Ability to gain a larger perspective than one's own personal faith integration

In this section we have looked at those overarching faith development processes of affiliating with one's inherited faith, of personalizing one's own faith, and of integrating the two outcomes together for a stable faith as an adult. The processes often overlap, and these are times when one feels pushed and pulled by various forces. These are also the times of most intense growth and change. For the church not to be a caring and active presence from the early teen years through the midtwenties is to abdicate the opportunity to have an influence when most faith shaping is to occur.

The Second Posture: Developmental Faith-Shaping Tasks of the Adolescent

"Faith Shaping," as the term is used in this book, does not refer to all phases of faith development, but it refers particularly to those adolescent and young adult years when most persons are actively involved in the task of giving shape and substance to their own personal faith. *Faith shaping is the process of acquiring one's own faith.*

Faith shaping includes *a sequence of tasks* through which young persons pass as they acquire their own faith. These tasks are not unlike the developmental tasks which have been identified by educators:

> A developmental task is a task which arises at or about a certain period in the life of an individual, successful achievement of which leads to his happiness and to success with later tasks, while failure leads to unhappiness in the individual, disapproval by the society, and difficulty with later tasks.[1]

Out of my own pastoral and personal experience I have identified seven tasks which I have seen youth encounter as they shape their faith. I call them *Faith-Shaping Tasks*. These tasks do not describe levels of maturity but, rather, the "work" that one must do to develop personal faith.

The Faith-Shaping Tasks

The seven tasks are in sequence, and most youth will work on the first task before the second and so forth. However, one's passage through the tasks will not occur at an even pace. Some persons will linger longer at one task. Some will delay beginning the faith tasks at all. Some will merge several tasks together while others slide back.

Most adolescents will work forward through these tasks in sequence. However, once they have worked through one task, they will return to that task many more times as they develop and mature in their faith. In truth, these tasks are a continual part of growth, and though faith shaping will lose much of its intensity, many adults work on these faith-shaping tasks throughout their lives. Indeed, if an adult is to keep

[1] Robert J. Havighurst, *Developmental Tasks and Education* (New York: David McKay Co., Inc., 1952), p. 2.

maturing in the faith, then work on these shaping tasks is essential. No one ever "completes" the tasks. The only thing final in life's development is death, and Christians don't even feel death is final. We feel that death is only the next step of maturation and development.

Faith-Shaping Task #1: *Experiencing*

Youth years are often filled with intense religious feelings. Spiritual emotions can be sporadic, spontaneous, and superficial. They are also the driving force behind the faith development of youth. Without this wellspring of emotions, faith shaping would lack power. Thus, it is important to recognize that providing a continual reservoir of spiritual feelings is an integral aspect of all faith shaping that will occur. A teenager who has had few religious stirrings is one who has not really entered the faith-shaping process. Religious experiences can happen in worship, at camps, on outings, while serving others, while singing together, through personal sharing, or at times of quiet retreat.

Nearly all youth have such experiences, though youth who are open to them will obviously have more.

Warm feelings of belonging, of being a part of a family of faith, of appreciation for being loved and accepted and included are all quite frequently associated with this introductory task. The desire to affiliate with the church is often a spiritual emotion. This desire can often be nothing more than an introductory religious stirring which needs to be complemented by more serious maturation.

Faith-Shaping Task #2: *Categorizing*

A person enters adolescence with bits and pieces of experiences, of memories, of ideas, and of thoughts. One of the tasks of adolescence is to make some understandable sense of these fragments by pulling them together into more of a whole. This sorting out is often the work of an inquisitive mind. The categories used by youth in early adolescence are frequently simplistic. Their religious thinking might be definite, yet naive. As individuals mature, they return to the task of categorizing. New experiences will cause more sophisticated thinking.

Categorizing is more than an intellectual exercise. Bits and pieces of emotions, attitudes, values, and intentions are also involved in this task. Any effort to consolidate emotions, clarify values, form a coherent memory, or shape an attitude is an effort to categorize experience.

Faith-Shaping Task #3: *Choosing*

Choosing is deciding: "What's important to me?" or "I like this and not that." In choosing is the role of valuing, deciding, and shaping a belief.

Choosing is a natural result of categorizing. After a new idea or experience is comprehended, the teenager chooses it, or believes it. Choosing might have long-term consequences, or it might be quite transitory with adolescents. In faith development, choosing is that time when a young person decides what is true for him or her. Yet the young person has not invested himself or herself in this new idea or truth. He or she is still rather detached from it. For example, in choosing, the young person could decide, "God is good," "Life can be trusted," and "God created the world."

Faith-Shaping Task #4: *Claiming*

In faith development, claiming happens when a young person decides to What or to Whom she or he will be true. Claiming is committing one's self to one's choices. Conversion is an act of claiming, of dedicating one's self to follow through on one's choices.

With an adolescent, choosing, categorizing, and experiencing continue, even after faith has been claimed. The youth is still weighing options and valuing. Generally, claiming has quite a cathartic effect. There is a sense of pride and satisfaction at having arrived at an important milestone. It is often a rich, emotional experience. Sometimes, when young people engage in claiming, they gain a feeling that they "have arrived," become overconfident and, therefore, closed.

Faith-Shaping Task #5: *Deepening*

This is the task of growing in the faith—of deepening conviction, commitment, and understanding. Often a teenager will not advance in this area until some time has intervened from the first act of claiming. When some of the newness of commitment has rubbed off and new questions arise, deepening is the task that confronts the person.

The task of deepening is one of working again through the earlier tasks of choosing and claiming, experiencing and categorizing. One is concerned to "update," or replace, naive thinking and commitment. Sometimes the deepening is called honest doubt; others can cause it to be guilt-ridden doubt. There is a great deal of irregularity in the pace of the deepening of one's faith. People grow in unique ways. When deepening occurs in an older adolescent, the overconfidence and "overcertainty" that might have marked the claiming task begin to take on a more mature perspective. Shades of "gray" are seen as opposed to the straight "black and white."

Faith-Shaping Task #6: *Separating*

This task is perhaps most characteristic of older adolescents and young adults. This is the task of setting aside commitments for a time. If an adolescent has worked through the first five tasks, chances are some space will be needed during post-high-school years in which to let one's faith set as well as settle. Distance and perspective are now needed. Other alternatives of faith often need to be examined and compared. Rebellion often marks this task. Some youth will swing far away from their roots, as in a pendulum, before resuming a more balanced stance. This distancing is with many young people a necessary task before they can work at synthesizing their rebellion with their roots and enter again the prior faith-shaping tasks.

Rather than being surprised or disturbed by this separating, rather than labeling it apathy or calling into question the earlier religious activity, one needs to recognize it as a legitimate faith task.

Faith-Shaping Task #7: *Responding*

This is the task of gaining a sense of one's life calling. Here is where one's mission or unique life purpose is considered. What informs this decision is the successful completion of the earlier faith-shaping tasks. For this to be a mature decision, a great deal of deepening and at least some separating should have occurred.

At the conclusion of the separating task and the beginning of the responding task, the young person is working hard on developing a new synthesis between newfound ideas and those ideas traditional to his or her upbringing. The synthesis spurs a new intensity of growth. Sometimes people call this a "second conversion," or a rebirth. It is a renewed commitment at a much deeper level. One feels a need to respond with one's life.

As a responder, these questions are considered: "Where is my calling in life? What have I to give? What can I offer to others and to

God? What special role is there for me? Where is my giftedness?''

It is a rare adolescent who enters this task. No adolescent should be pushed into this stage. It is a developmental task far more typical of young adults, though some adolescents will venture into responding.

The "Late Bloomers"

The truth is that some youth will never move beyond the task of experiencing, or even very far into the task of experiencing. They have simply not matured to the point where the shaping of faith is a personal priority. I recall one young boy who was an active participant in my church. His parents were active in all facets of the church. But he simply had not reached the stage of religious experiences, even when he was a senior in high school. He wasn't a slow learner, and he was quite popular with other youth. But he was slow to take responsibility, and he wasn't, at this stage of his life, a very thoughtful or deep person. His situation is not all that rare among youth.

We must accept this. These youth will need to wait until young adulthood before they begin to work on the faith-shaping tasks. And that is all right. For what they develop will probably stand more firmly when done at a more mature age. These "late bloomers" may not have to work through the task of separating.

Adult Responsibilities Relating to Faith-Shaping Tasks

Task #1: *Experiencing* (spiritual feelings)

Try to provide for open-ended expression of feeling.
Encourage feelings that lead to something further.
Allow youth to express themselves openly.
Provide for rich feeling experiences.
Model with your own feelings.
Don't ever let it stop with feelings. As the teenager is ready, encourage him or her to move to the next task.

Task #2: *Categorizing* (sorting out feelings, values, experiences, memories)

Do concept studies on Christian ideas. Don't do the work for youth, but provide some handles.
Be a person who can be trusted.
Never ridicule ideas, no matter how ludicrous they appear.
Be accepting. Don't take everything too seriously.
Be affirming, but do provide honest feedback. You don't need to agree dishonestly with everything uttered.

Task #3: *Choosing* (deciding what is true to me)

Encourage youth to think. Challenge them!
Model your own values and choices.
Focus discussions on beliefs that can be prized.
Teach youth how to doubt creatively, and they'll arrive at more authentic beliefs.

Task #4: *Claiming* (deciding to What I will be true)

Plan many invitations to commitment in a variety of settings.
Talk to youth individually and intimately about their own decisions of claiming.
Plan appropriate times of celebration when claiming occurs.
Be certain to provide follow-up support after claiming.
Don't treat claiming as an end in itself but as one step in a lifelong process.
Develop young people's open-mindedness.

Task #5: *Deepening* (maturing in the faith)

For youth who are ready, provide appropriate intellectual stimulus.
Don't have high expectations here.
Don't push too soon after conversion. Allow for some "settling in" time.
Share the depth of your faith, your struggles, your questions, your growing edge.
Be a helping and enabling person. Undergird youth with your prayers and support.

Task #6: *Separating* (setting aside faith for a time)

Don't be disappointed or fret unnecessarily as this occurs.
You should express honest reactions, but do give freedom and space to the "separated" youth.
Never let this sever relationships. Open and trusting communication is the greatest witness. Keep in touch!
Work with parents and others affected by their own sense of guilt, despair, or failure. Help them to see the naturalness of this step.
Celebrate new growth as it occurs.

Task #7: *Responding* (commitment to a life calling)

Encourage this when the person is ready. Initiate only with great sensitivity.

Portray callings as "glimpses" and "visions" rather than facts
or certainties.
Study gifts and prayer/meditation with youth.
Always affirm and lift up what you see as a person's gifts,
abilities, and talents.
Provide opportunities for youth to develop their God-given
potential and talents.
Provide a warm and positive atmosphere for persons to ex-
periment with their own mission and purpose in life.

Adults and the Diversity of the Faith-Shaping Tasks

"How do adults relate with young people at widely varied stages?"

Bill is a senior high church school teacher and a highly regarded
one. He is evaluating his last class session with another adult sponsor:
"Why is it that this morning's discussion on death and eternal life
turned on Susan and Dick and turned off all the others? We had a
discipline problem with two of our younger boys, but Susan and Dick
just couldn't seem to get enough of it."

The answer could be simple enough: Susan and Dick could be
working through the Faith-Shaping Tasks on a different level than the
other youth. To Susan and Dick, the "remote" subject of death and
eternal life is important, because they have already experienced, ca-
tegorized, chosen, and claimed a faith that deals somewhat maturely
with life and daily concerns. Now they are able to venture out into
these more distant issues. The other adolescents in the group might
include some who have barely begun the faith: shaping tasks, others
who would rationalize the entire subject with a naive doctrine, and
others who are consumed with more immediate life issues.

What the Faith-Shaping Tasks teach us is to consider youth uniquely. There is no need to become overly concerned that we are not talented
enough as adult leaders to attract each person's attention to any given
subject. The Faith-Shaping Tasks also teach that we need to have
individual and private times with youth. Group times are necessary
because youth learn a great deal from socializing with one another. But
they also need one-on-one times with adults to work carefully on a
personal agenda in a trusting environment.

How do we work with a group of youth at widely varied stages?
I would suggest five responses:

1. Think of the diversity as being positive. Because of it, youth

can learn from one another. More mature youth are often the best teachers.

2. Don't fret about it. It would be unusual for members of a group to be at the same stage working on the same tasks. Often adults unknowingly use the pressures of group socialization to force a youth group to function at the level of the group's most active and verbal leaders, or at the level in which the adults are most comfortable.

3. Find private times to be with each young person for authentic and deep conversation. Do it regularly.

4. Help the youth to appreciate the diversity and the different concerns each of them brings to the group.

5. Train adults so that they do not expect or strive for uniformity. Adults need to be able to develop an atmosphere where youth are set free to learn from one another and to be able to experience significant dialogue with adult models. Adults need to be trained to recognize the Faith-Shaping Tasks and to help youth as they work through them.

An example might be in order to illustrate these responses. Several years ago, an adolescent named Frank came into our church with his parents. They had not been in church recently, and one of the reasons for his parents' return was because of Frank's problems in their previous community. He had been in trouble with the law, at school, with drugs, and with his parents. Both Frank and his parents saw coming into our community as an opportunity to begin anew.

Frank was a great deal different from the other youth in our group. He had seen a side of life they had never experienced. Frank learned a great deal from the more established youth during his first year. He also had a great deal to offer them from his varied experiences.

In the following years, Frank developed a thoughtful faith. He was balanced, helpful, and insightful. I talked with him personally many times. Finally, I approached Frank about church membership and Christian baptism. He was interested and seemed to understand all the ramifications. He asked solid questions and seemed satisfied with the conclusions he reached.

For some reason in the months that followed he could not make a public decision of faith. As I thought about it, I realized that Frank had worked through the Faith-Shaping Tasks perhaps too smoothly for a person with no church background. I began to wonder if he had sped through his own spiritual development "to be like the other kids." I realized that Frank had a very low level of self-esteem and guilt because of his background in the previous community.

On a retreat one night, Frank and I definitely had occasion to discuss this. I said to him, "Frank, I've been wondering if you think you're worthy enough to call yourself a Christian. Do you think you deserve God's love?" No sooner had I said the words than tears and violent weeping began. A sensitive chord had been touched. In the corner of that lodge, Frank learned about grace. I shared with him my belief that no one deserved God's love. I told him that I had done enough harmful things in my life to keep me forever from the kingdom of love. Only God's undeserved graciousness makes the relationship possible. In dialogue, we both began to understand the hurts of those memories within Frank and how they inhibited him from internalizing what had been so publicly and easily affirmed.

Frank's experience illustrates how diversity among youth and the varied ways youth work through the Faith-Shaping Tasks can be positive. Frank learned a great deal from the group and the group learned from Frank. At the beginning, we constantly had to help the other youth accept Frank and his uniqueness. Yet it was the private times with Frank that finally penetrated and spurred him to a deeper maturity of faith. Adults need to be trained to provide an atmosphere where positive faith shaping is encouraged.

The Third Posture: Readiness, the Way We Grow and Motivate Growth

In this chapter we have explored the processes of growth and the seven Faith-Shaping Tasks which persons must work through in order to shape a mature faith. We have recognized typical patterns of faith development.

What we have not discussed is what spurs human growth. *Our own readiness is what motivates and determines our growth.* We desire stability and balance in our lives. We want things to be in order and in perspective. We want to be able to understand, interpret, and react maturely to all of life's experiences. No person ever fully attains this desired level of balance. Because we cannot and do not, we are constantly bumping up against our own limitations and inadequacies. We must develop a faith in Something that fits the "missing pieces" together. We must depend upon Someone to do for us what we cannot do for ourselves. This recognition of limits opens the way for faith. Interestingly enough, it is awareness of our limitations and inadequacies that not only provides our need for faith but also provides for growth. When our lives get out of balance, when we are most restless and dissatisfied, when we enter into a crisis, when we are striving or seeking after something difficult to attain, when we become most aware of our personal potential or an unexplored ability are the times when growth is likely to occur.

Developmental scientists call this phenomenon "readiness." Reading readiness has to do with the level of reading a student is ready to grasp. Religious readiness has to do with the level of faith a person is ready to grasp. To ascertain one's readiness is to take one's own "growth temperature."

The dictionary defines "ready" as "prepared for use or for action. Prepared in mind; willing." [1] Our readiness determines to what we are open:

• to what and to whom we will be receptive,
• in what we will be prepared and willing to engage ourselves,
• in what ways we will be expectant,
• in what directions our hopes and longings will lie,
• and, for Christians, in what direction is God leading.

To be ready for marriage means that I am willing to enter into its commitments. To be ready for college expresses my eagerness to be receptive to what a college has to offer. To be ready to die means that I have come to terms with my own existence and am prepared to meet whatever death holds for me.

Readiness can be seen as a tension, a stirring, a dissatisfaction, a striving, a push from within. Readiness can be determined within a person by developmental limits, intellectual ability, physical ability, emotional maturity, motivation, personal habits, attitude and mood, expectation of others, and spiritual receptivity.

The growth of faith in youth can be traced to their level of readiness: Is the young person ready to be confronted with this moral question? Is she or he ready to make this faith decision? Does this young person want to learn this biblical concept? What is she or he seeking? What troubles her or him?

[1] Funk and Wagnalls, *Standard College Dictionary* (New York: Funk & Wagnalls Co., 1966).

Human development is really God's timing. God surely is not constricted to our measures of hours, days, minutes, or years. God's "time" is set within us by the tempo of our own development. The stirrings and proddings within us are divinely created and inspired. It is never wrong or sinful to get in touch with one's own readiness. *For to be in touch with the direction of one's growth is to be in touch with God's creative leading.*

God is not in a hurry to bring us to maturity . . .
    He has forever . . .
    The process is eternal.
    We get hung up on time limitations . . .
    As though everything has to happen today.
Despite our profession of faith in life after death,
we live much of the time as though everything has to
happen this side of the grave . . .
Victims of the visible . . .
    Bound by the tangible . . .
    The tyranny of time and space.
The fact is—the infinite, eternal, unchangeable God is directing the believer's maturation process.
    Growing into His image takes a lot longer than three
    score years and ten . . .
    The best of us—by the time he reaches the grave—
    still has a long way to go.
Perfection is not so much a goal as it is a relationship.
    To be humanly perfect is to be right with God and
    right with one another.
    Love is the nearest thing to perfection.
    "God is love."
    "He that loves is born of God."
    "He that does not love does not know God."—1 John 4.
Patience and love are the marks of the disciple—patience in God's faithfulness and love for Him and others. [2]

The apostle Paul understood readiness, and he wrote of it directly. In his first letter to the Corinthians, he wrote, "As a matter of fact, my brothers, I could not talk to you as I talk to people who have the Spirit; I had to talk to you as though you belonged to this world, as children in the Christian faith. I had to feed you milk, not solid food, because you were not ready for it. And even now you are still not ready for it,

[2] Richard C. Halverson, "Perspective," *Faith at Work*, August, 1977, p. 29, italics added. Reprinted by permission from Faith at Work, 11065 Little Patuxent Pkwy., Columbia, MD 21044.

because you still live as the people of this world live" (1 Corinthians 3:1-3a, TEV).

The danger we encounter in talking of human development is that we have to generalize and talk about what is typical. Readiness balances that danger by focusing upon what the individual is uniquely and peculiarly ready to encounter.

Our task in youth ministry is to help youth envision faith as a lifelong journey of growth and maturation. This is a difficult assignment because they stand at the very beginning of the journey, and from their vantage, it does not seem like a journey. In far too many churches we unconsciously communicate that faith is a onetime decision completed by baptism or confirmation. Churches of all theological persuasion are guilty.

Since faith and growth both arise as we become more aware of our limitations, faith and growth have a very special relationship to one another. A living faith is one that continually ascertains the next step of growth and attains it. A dead faith is one in which there is no awareness of what one is ready to learn or to experience.

Faith rarely arises out of our feeling adequate about ourselves and in control of our life and world. Faith arises out of our inadequacies, our limits, our finiteness, our seeking something greater than we ourselves are. Faith relates a person or community to their limiting boundaries and to the potential of their experience. A truly faithful community is one that lives at its potential. At the outer limits, faith pushes a person to the tension of readiness, to the tension of growth. Dynamic faith for youth or adults is living on the frontierland of our convictions, hopes and experiences. Moses, Abraham, Isaiah, Amos, Paul, Mary, and Jesus are all remembered because their faith related them to the limiting boundaries of their lives. They lived "on life's edges."

We must be sensitive to the unique readiness of each young person. Not all we do can be tailor-made for each individual. But neither must we lump all youth together and treat them as identical. The faith needs of one youth will vary greatly from those of another.

How do youth acquire faith? Surely the first appropriate response is that there exists no "one way" to acquire faith. There are as many paths to faith as there are faithful Christians. Who is to say which is best, or who acquired faith in the most mature way? Augustine did not acquire the faith, even though his devout mother attempted to nurture him, until he had spent years in reckless living. However, after he did repent, his life and faith became a beacon to many. We would not advocate that pattern, but we would be foolish to condemn it also.

When a young person is ready to develop faith, let us be there, ready to respond to her or his needs. When a young person needs to be reminded of her or his own potential, or limitations, let us be willing to challenge her or him lovingly, so as to spur personal growth.

Our faith becomes profound when, in the words of Bishop Stephen Neill of India, we "commit all that we know of ourselves to all that we know of God." That is all that we are ever asked to do.

Chapter 5

Basics
and
Beginnings

To nurture children in the faith is to help them develop proper handles, tools, and memories so that when they actively engage as adolescents in faith shaping, they will have the needed ingredients to develop a mature faith.

THE BASICS APPROACH: an attempt by adults to present a "simplified adult faith" to children

THE BEGINNINGS APPROACH: an attempt by adults to present an appropriate grounding and foundation for children, to be used in future faith development

We cannot understand what must happen in faith development with youth until we comprehend what must happen in this area with children. One age truly is the foundational stone for the other. What we try to accomplish in faith development with youth is built directly upon what we accomplish with children.

There is and must be a substantive difference between the faith nurturing of children and that of youth. The childhood years are the storing, collecting, incubating years. Adolescents use those foundations to internalize, personalize, or shape their faith.

The Two Approaches with Children

The most effective method of faith development with children is a foundational method I call the *Beginnings Approach*. The beginnings style emphasizes bringing faith near to children, rather than directly, until they are developmentally ready to respond to the directness.

The more familiar approach, however, I call the *Basics Approach*. Many adults, so influenced by the desire to evangelize children, believe that the most effective approach is a full presentation of the gospel as early as possible. They reason that the younger one is who claims the faith, the better. They believe we should bring children both "nearly" and "directly" to the story of faith.

The *Basics Approach* is characterized by these assumptions:

1. Children need to be presented with the gospel as completely and as early as possible. They need to be taught the simple basics and fundamentals of adult belief and doctrine.

2. Children have a need for a personal faith. They are capable of accepting or rejecting the gospel. They are ready to enter into the Faith-Shaping Tasks of Claiming and Choosing.

3. The best way for children to learn about faith is for it to be told to them directly, clearly, and unashamedly.

4. The best way to respond to children's questions and strivings is to answer them once and for all.

5. The emphasis in childhood is upon constructing a faith.

These assumptions sound reasonable and helpful. It is upon these assumptions that much of our faith development with children is now based.

The *Beginnings Approach* has another, quite different, set of assumptions:

1. The emphasis in childhood is upon preparing for faith. It is a time to prepare a repertoire of memories rich in faith potential. It is a time to bring faith and its traditions near to children.

2. Children do not yet have a need for adult faith. They have not yet experienced real uncertainties or limitations about themselves. They do not have a firm grasp of their heritage, experiences, or memories. Adolescence is normally the earliest age at which they enter into in-

tentional faith shaping, taking responsibility for their lives.

3. Children will sometimes want to covenant with their church in a desire for affiliation and belonging, but making lifelong commitments is normally an adolescent or adult task.

4. Children need to be presented with beginnings to faith: isolated handles, tantalizers, feelings, concepts, tools, and memories to be used at a later age to form a personal faith. Complete formulations are confusing to children. They tend to think with more immediacy, in bits and pieces. They do not have the connecting, summarizing, or theologizing ability of adults.

5. Faith is not a set dogma or creed to be accepted or rejected. It is something that needs to be personalized by each believer; ". . . religion is not something grafted superficially onto the personality; religion is what the whole person becomes by its growth. . . ." [1]

6. Formal learning needs to be responsive to the readiness of the individual. Providing answers to questions that have not and are not being asked can be smothering to future growth.

Let's consider Easter as it would be presented in both approaches. In the Basics Approach, we would not only tell children the story and chronology of events of Jesus' life at Easter but also expect them to parrot back to us the doctrinal meaning of these events. The Beginnings Approach to Easter would develop concepts of death, life, sacrifice, miracle, surprise, and courage. We could act out stories of Jesus' courtroom scenes and Peter's denial. We could experience the celebration of Jesus as a loser and as a victor and what that means in the child's experience. We would tell the stories of the crucifixion and resurrection as stories, not as doctrine. We would follow up on any of the children's probings and allow them to come to their own conclusions. We would attempt to provide not a faith interpretation (that's the Basics) but, rather, an opportunity to provide ingredients for future faith interpretation.There would be another day, later in their maturity, to understand Easter.

Comparing the Two Approaches

When we look at our children, we see they are unspoiled, innocent, and easily influenced. Children seem so eager to please and to be

[1] R. S. Lee, *Your Growing Child and Religion* (New York: Macmillan, Inc., 1963), pp. 136-137.

obedient to adult will. Faith commitments "appear" to be so much easier for children than for adolescents. This is because the teenagers have so many more things to consider when they enter into a faith commitment. *We must be careful to provide children with what they need rather than what we want.*

In our faith we should not be apologetic: We would like for our daughters and sons to accept faith in our Lord Jesus Christ. We would like for them to accept our faith bias.

And so, what do we do? Shall we present our children with the gospel so true, simple, and constant down through the centuries? Shall we present the basics of the gospel directly to children? What else can we do?

Presenting children directly with the "simple and complete gospel" is not only inadequate but also inappropriate if we are hoping for them seriously to accept the gospel later in life when they are more able to do so.

Too often we have wanted to convert children on our time schedules instead of allowing God to do the converting on God's natural developmental "time schedule." We structure Christian education for children as if they are "little adults" because we are afraid they will miss what we have to tell them. We do so because of our lack of faith in God. We are unwilling to give to God what is important to us: our children. Yet our children are not created in our image but in God's image. God is the only keeper of the clock of readiness. Persons are ready for different challenges at each stage of life. Everything has a season (see Ecclesiastes 3).

If I were to teach an adult who has never heard of Christianity, I would tell him the very basics of my faith—what it means to me and what it can mean to him. I would use the simplest and most basic words. I would teach him Christian symbols and their meanings. But an adult has capabilities that children do not.

To nurture children in the faith is to help them develop proper handles, tools, and memories so that when they actively engage as adolescents in faith shaping, they will have the needed ingredients to develop a mature faith. This is the Beginnings Approach because it stresses that a personalized faith can have its beginnings in the childhood years but will be given substance only as the child moves into and beyond adolescence.

What can happen to children educated by the Basics Approach?

1. They will probably get answers before they have questions, and thus when they do naturally ask their own questions of faith, the answers they have received will sound antique and trite.

2. They might conclude that Christianity is complicated and unreal, that faith is unrelated to the real concerns of life.

3. Since they will find it nearly impossible to be true to a faith commitment at their age, they might learn an artificial separation between belief and behavior.

4. Later in life some will feel that they have been exploited and manipulated in having been encouraged to join the church and profess faith. The decision they made will now lack meaning, and thus faith will lack meaning.

5. They will have received Basics at such an early and superficial stage that some will never be able to extend their faith to a deeper level, even in their adult years. It will be frozen and hollow.

What can happen to children nurtured by the Beginnings Approach?

1. Their curiosity will be whetted. They can arrive at adolescence with questions that have not yet been answered!

2. They can learn earlier that faith must be personalized and internalized. No one else can do it for them.

3. As adolescents, they will likely be ready emotionally, volitionally, and developmentally to engage in faith shaping. They will have been given the proper skills and tools to engage in the task.

4. They may be willing as children to make a covenant with their church to be "beginners in faith."

5. They can discover the church and Christianity to be rich in human experience, natural, and a part of their real world.

If we conclude that the Beginnings Approach is most appropriate, what happens to the Basics? We cannot and should not dismiss the Basics. The youngest children need to see adult faith in action. They need to hear it preached, see it demonstrated, and modeled as a possible goal for themselves. *They need to be near Basics but not have the approach aimed directly at them.*

The Shape of the Beginnings Approach

Let's explore the specifics about what Beginnings in faith development can mean. What will it look like in church education?

It will be focused on developing these handles, experiences, and tools that children can use as they mature:

1. *Bible Stories.* In the Beginnings we are not striving for a holistic understanding of the Bible. We do, however, want children to be very familiar and comfortable with the Bible. We should emphasize those parts they can easily understand: parables, stories, and incidents rather than highly symbolic passages (e.g., emphasize Paul's travels, actions, and personality rather than his theological formulations). The Bible will become a loved book full of exciting incidents, real people, and an exciting and real God. It will not seem distant, hard to read, or complicated. In the Beginnings Approach, the child's interpretations will be accepted and nurtured.

2. *Adult Faith as a Model.* Children can observe the faith of adults in worship, in congregational life, in mission, and use it as a model for their own faith development.

3. *Concept Education.* Children need to develop key Christian concepts which are a basic part of the foundation for a future faith. It is essential to refine such concepts as life, love, sharing, caring, death, right and wrong, hope, honesty, joy, peace, anger, pride, power, wonder, God, the Bible, church, and promise. Their curriculum could help them explore a concept by reading about it, acting it out, playing games based upon it, "crafting" things from it, relating it to life, and testing it upon life.

4. *The Child's Natural Ability to Wonder, to Question, to Create, to Imagine, and to Initiate.* Helping children be creative, imaginative, and curious will give them specific skills to use in faith shaping as adolescence approaches.

5. *A Rehearsal at Interpreting Life's Experiences.* Children are very curious. They often ask "Why?" "How?" and "When?" Practice at interpretation of experiences is the beginning of a faith-shaping skill. Encourage their interpretation skills.

6. *A Rich Repertoire of Memories.* Use the same variety of memories as suggested for youth in chapter 3: headline experiences, repetition experiences, personally touching events, and significant relationships. The patterns of nearness are similar for children and youth.

7. *A Warm, Inviting, Welcoming Family of Faith.* Such a church family affirms children where they are and with integrity launches them

on a lifelong journey in which they became persons of faith.

Summary

Emphasis on basic doctrinal interpretations can be counterproductive because the memory is formed by the child and not us. If we force doctrine, all the child might remember is the unpleasantness with which we forced the issue. Many post-high-school youth who have grown up in the church feel unpleasant impressions. Many of those who have experienced faith development from the Basics Approach feel faith to be manipulative, adult dominated, irrelevant, undesirable, and stilted.

Beginnings to faith can be offered to children in the context of an adult community of faith. They will see and hear the Basics from that adult community, but they will not be expected to embrace all that basic faith represents for adults.

There are some churches that are guilty of never allowing children to see or witness the Basics of adult faith. These are the churches that separate the children from the adult community when it worships, studies, and fellowships. There are homes where children are taught to pray the familiar childhood prayers but never hear authentic prayers from their parents.

Children need to experience an *introduction to faith* (Beginnings) while at the same time experience the *destination of their faith journey: adult faith* (Basics). It is no better to clobber children with exclusive Basics than to "underwhelm" them with exclusive Beginnings.

Good church school curriculum emphasizes Basics for the first time in the junior high years. This is the appropriate time for the faith to be presented directly. What a joy it is to be able to present the story of Christian faith when adolescents have spent their childhood years in preparation for it! What a joy not to find the terrain cluttered with earlier attempts to push religious commitment ahead of God's natural timing!

Beginnings are a tool of nearness and should be emphasized during the childhood years as the foundation upon which the Basics of faith can be presented—fresh, alive, and new, when adolescents are most able to embrace faith.

Chapter 6

Giftedness: A Unique Faith-Shaping Agenda

Teenagers should be developing their minds, talents, bodies, and feelings. They should be developing their capacity to relate, to create, to search, to give thanks. With the proper mind-set, these are all acts of a developing faith.

GIFTEDNESS: all of the personal resources with which God has endowed you

The Faith-Shaping Task of Responding (discovering one's life calling) has its roots in giftedness. In chapter 4, the task of Responding was described as primarily a young adult task. Yet this important Faith-Shaping Task is motivated and enriched by an emphasis in the teen years upon giftedness.

Giftedness is all the ways that God has invested divine nature in each human life. Faith in God and giftedness are partner convictions. If we enter into a relationship with the God of love, then the next step of faith is to believe that this God has endowed us with many resources for the living of our lives. God created us and endowed us! All personal resources which we enjoy and use are thus seen as gifts from God.

When Youth Understand Their Giftedness

Youth enhance their faith reservoir by developing their God-given giftedness. *If youth understand their talents, resources, and abilities as gifts* (not "I am talented" but "I am gifted"), *then the unfolding of God's investment within them is a matter of faith development.*

Faith involves more than a private, spiritual endeavor. Faith involves the unfolding of the totality of one's life and being. *Christian faith is coming to know* (1) *how God has invested in us* and (2) *how we can invest ourselves in God's way.* Faith ultimately requires responding to the direction of God's leading.

The teen years are a prime time, perhaps *the* prime time of life, to begin to see one's personal resources as gifts and to explore the meaning of those gifts.

Our personal resources are primarily interior, i.e., what is within us. However, our resources also include what's exterior: body, possessions, environment, etc. For the teen, standing at the edge of adult life, most of the resources will be one's own person (not belongings, status, or possessions)—body, mind, personality, talents, skills, interests, volitions, creativity, initiative, inclinations, dreams, expectations, behavior, self-discipline, and feelings.

The development of these personal resources *can be* a faith-shaping task. The popular or humanistic understanding of these resources would be to view them as "happenstance" or as "something one has deserved or earned," or as "something innately human," or as "that which makes one unique," or as "that which one has inherited or acquired." Some of these observations might be partly accurate.

But Christians, on the other hand, view these resources as gifts. Christians see them as undeserved gifts from a loving God who has freely *endowed* human life with *potential.* God gives the raw materials of personality and ability; God gives the undeveloped capacity to feel, to develop physically, to uncover our talents.

If we view our personal resources as unearned gifts, if we understand that a loving God has given them to us with the divine intention that they be developed and used for the right purposes, then we are likely to feel both grateful and energized.

We will not feel cocky or conceited with all the resources we were smart enough to acquire. We acknowledge that they are gifts to us.

We will not feel cheated when we see someone else excel where we do not, because we realize the individuality of giftedness. We excel in ways they do not.

We will not feel selfish as we realize that what we have is not to be used only for our own desires, lusts, or ambitions.

We will not feel alone, thinking no one truly knows our potential or understands how it can be used.

If young persons begin to understand their giftedness, they are learning God's plan for their lives; they are beginning a lifetime of thankfulness for all that has been so freely given to them.

Teenagers should be developing their minds, talents, bodies, and feelings. They should be developing their capacity to relate, to create, to search, to give thanks. With the proper mind-set these are all acts of a developing faith.

Nothing is more exciting than to see a teenager sing her first solo and with pride realize, "I'm good!"—Nothing more exciting than to watch a young girl practice for hours and months and finally make the school basketball team!—Nothing more exciting than to see a son bring home his first painting from art class!—Nothing more exciting than to see a new bit of wisdom arise from the ashes of a first broken relationship. God must surely smile at those times, watching the development of divine creation!

The development of one's gifts is one of the most important tasks of adolescence. If we discourage teenagers and thwart their potential, they will carry a scar for the rest of their days. Consider how much time young persons spend each and every day developing their gifts! One young girl I know, while perhaps not typical, attends modern dance rehearsal after school four times a week. She now teaches younger ones to dance. She plays the clarinet and rehearses and performs at that extensively. She is taking an advance level weekly piano lesson. She's holding down her first job, developing abilities as a responsible employee. She attends high school full-time, developing intellectual abilities. She dates and participates actively in the church fellowship group, pruning and shaping her relational skills. She interacts frequently with adults in the church community, thereby learning that ability. She sings in the church choir and participates in the bell choir with other youth. Many youth spend extraordinary amounts of time and energy developing their giftedness. It perhaps is one of the most common traits of adolescence.

Gospel Logic About Giftedness

I have always felt that we place the emphasis in the wrong place in the story of Jesus' feeding the five thousand by the shores of the Sea of Galilee. We look at the little lad with five loaves and two fishes, at his willingness, and we look at the miracle, Jesus' expanding the food.

The point of the story often missed is to be found by looking at the disciples. The incident happens early-on in the disciples' ministry, according to the account in Mark's Gospel. Jesus had sent the disciples out for the first time, two by two, to minister and preach in nearby towns. It is obvious they are inexperienced by the elemental instructions Jesus gives them. The subsequent beheading of John the Baptist must have left them feeling insecure and fearful.

When they return from their ministry in nearby towns and villages, they are weary and tired. So they climb into a boat, and Jesus takes them to a remote area to get away and relax. But the crowds race on ahead of them; so anxious are they to see Jesus! And Jesus has such compassion on the waiting crowd that he set aside the weariness of the disciples for the needs of the people. A long day went by, full of crowds pushing and pressing against Jesus and his tired disciples. On such days the disciples probably did little more than attempt to manage the crowds, assist Jesus, and troubleshoot all the inevitable problems.

As the day wore on, the disciples came to Jesus, worried, and said, "This is a lonely place. These people need food. Send them away." And Jesus said, "Give them something to eat." (Jesus obviously knew the disciples had no physical food at their disposal.) And the disciples replied sarcastically, "Do you want us to spend a life's savings to feed these people dinner?" But Jesus was concerned with more than food.

So he asked them, "How much do you have? Go and see." And the disciples went out and looked only for that which satisfies physical hunger. They looked for material food. And they brought back five loaves and two fishes from a small lad. Even amidst their searching, these were all the resources that they could find. Jesus sighed. "Get these people seated." And he looked up to heaven and asked a blessing,

"Father, bless the food that satisfies soul and body." And he broke the bread, and in the breaking of the bread and the distributing of the fish, the food expanded to fill the need.

Scripture says, "[The disciples] were completely dumbfounded, for they had not understood the incident of the loaves. Their minds were closed" (Mark 6:52, NEB).

Jesus sensed the people's spiritual needs, and he sensed the people's physical needs, and he could not and did not separate the two. And he saw that it was his mission to meet the needs of the body and soul and to ask of those who were his disciples, "In the midst of the needs of this world, how much do you have?"

Jesus was attempting to teach his own disciples in this incident. First, he had challenged them to go out, two by two, with no other resources than that of their own faith and their own abilities. Then, he challenged them to respond on faith to the needs of the crowd. He wanted them to see beyond the puniness of the five loaves and two fishes to the majesty and wonder of food to feed body and soul.

Jesus was attempting to be responsive to the giftedness of that moment; the disciples couldn't see beyond the frenzy of the moment.

Jesus was asking the disciples, "How has God gifted you for this moment? What resources has God laid at your disposal?" Most of us see our resources as *our* possessions, *our* talents, *our* skills. And so do youth. Jesus was asking his disciples to look at the very same resources and see them as gifts.

Giftedness is the point of this story! Giftedness is how much God has invested in our life. We were set forth on our earthly trek with the giftedness to be able to meet the demands of each day. And in this context, it is a sin not to recognize our gifts, or to develop our gifts, or to volunteer our gifts.

There was a difference between Jesus and his disciples on that remote hillside in the middle of a huge crowd. It was the difference between a frenzied, frantic, and worried group attempting to respond to the problems of the moment and a concerned, loving, receptive, prayerful person who on faith responded to those about him.

There's some "gospel logic" about giftedness that can be drawn from this story that has tremendous implications for youth, who, like the disciples, are young in their Christian experience. Jesus could just as well be teaching these five points about giftedness to youth today as he did to his disciples. (The word "have" is used here not to refer to the possessions but to the totality of what God has given to a person.)

1. *We have more than we think we do.*

The first premise of giftedness is that we are not in touch with all of the potential that God has given to us. Indeed, when we feel insecure or unworthy, we are often not aware of all the value, the esteem, and the giftedness God created in us. "He who sows sparingly will also reap sparingly, and he who sows bountifully will also reap bountifully" (2 Corinthians 9:6). The disciples were stuck because they could find only the obvious—five loaves and two fishes.

One of the most common traits of adolescents is insecurity about themselves: "Am I OK? Am I acceptable? Am I worthy?" These are critical life issues for youth. Jesus is telling them: "Your giftedness is far greater than you think it is." Youth are just beginning to uncover all of their talents and abilities. They are often at such tentative, tenuous stages of development. They are often reminded more of their limitations than their capabilities.

2. *The more we give, the more we have.*

That doesn't make any sense at all, and it never has. Jesus said it in Luke 6:38: "Give, and it will be given to you." In the youth musical "How Free Is Free?" the Fool, the main character, says these lines to the cast: "Oh . . . and don't forget to continue to look to your Father so that you can receive and understand more of Him, so that you can give more. . . . the more you receive [your giftedness], the more you have to give, and the more you give, the more you can receive." [1] This is the main point in the story of the feeding of the five thousand. The more we give, the more we have. The more open we are to God's giftedness, the more we have to share with others. Youth discover their purpose in life as they give of themselves to others.

3. *We've got to know what we have in order to give what we have.*

Jesus told the disciples, "Go and see how much you have." The disciples thought all they had was five loaves and two fishes. They didn't realize all the other resources available to them. How tiny youth think their own resources to be! Christians must be people continually becoming aware of their own giftedness: their own ability to share and

---

[1] "How Free Is Free?" a youth musical. Lyrics and script by Errol Strider, music by Michael Brandt. Property of Creative Spirit, Inc., 1520 Euclid Avenue, Boulder, Colorado 80302.

give, their talents and abilities. Youth need to be aware that when they are not growing in self-awareness and discovery, then they are not going in God's way.

4. *Our own gifts need to be called forth by others. They will recognize our gifts before we do.*

We must be people who call forth the gifts of one another—youth to youth, adult to youth, youth to adult. We must be intimate and honest enough with one another so that we can recognize a new ability bursting forth or see a promising new direction for service. Most of us are ignorant and blind to our own giftedness until someone else points us toward it. Whenever we call forth the gifts in others, we are allowing God to work through us. Youth are normally willing and open to allow others to call forth their gifts. We need only find more sensitive adults available to do it.

5. *The only way to use effectively what we have is to volunteer what we have.*

Matthew 10:8 (KJV) says, "Freely ye have received, freely give." Once when I came to a pastorate, someone took me aside and said, "People in this church really like to be asked to do things by the pastors. They'll respond if *you* ask them." That is an excuse for inaction! Worse yet, it is unbiblical! Certainly there are times when people need to be asked to do something because we are attempting to call forth their gifts. Jesus asked the disciples to go out two by two because he thought they would discover something exciting about their own ministries and abilities. But the more normative pattern in a church should be that people come forward to say, "I want to be used. I want to help." We're always so worried that people will think we're too conceited or pushy when we volunteer ourselves. Or we're frightened that if we volunteer to do one thing, the church will ask us to do everything else. Too many people are caught up with the question "What are *they* going to ask me to do?" rather than "How can I be of service? How can I put to work the resources God has given me?" Our words to youth will not do much good, but our actions will. Strong adult modeling will effectively communicate the right way for them.

When Jesus asked his disciples, "How much do you have?" he meant in that question all of these things. He meant to tell them, "You've got more than you think you do. If you'll give more, you'll receive more. You've got to 'go and see' what you have in order to

give what you have. If you'll trust me, I can call forth your giftedness.
I can see it more clearly from my vantage point than you can from
yours. And, finally, don't send the people to someone else to be fed;
feed them yourselves. Volunteer what you have to meet the physical
and spiritual needs of people.''

A PROCLAMATION OF GIFTEDNESS
A Paraphrase (Ephesians 1:3-10, 18-19)

PRAISE BE TO GOD, who has freely given us more than we need to
put our lives into proper order.

We have been fully endowed and gifted!

God decided at the beginning of the world that all human life would,
by definition, have purpose and value and be worthy of His Complete Love.

Our future and our destiny are to be discovered as we recognize ourselves as sons and daughters of God.

In Christ, that which imprisons us can be liberated.

Through Christ our mistakes, our limitations, and our guilt will be
completely forgiven.

God has been lavish with human beings, giving us full wisdom and
insight.

God has even made known to us the hidden purpose in creating this
world: namely, that the universe, all heaven and all earth, might
be brought into unity and wholeness because of the sacrifice of
His Son, Jesus Christ.

I pray that you might be given the inner vision to know:
  First, the future to which God is calling you;
  Second, the vast resources God offers to share with you if you believe
  in Him;
  Third, the power within us that God can make available.

Chapter 7

Contexts for Faith Nurturing

*When we speak of adolescent faith development, we must talk
of it inclusively, in a variety of settings. We must focus upon
all settings, for roots will only be deep and foundations only
secure if the faith of a young person is fed harmoniously and
consistently by all the contexts and relationships in which his
or her life is lived.*

In the remaining chapters of this book, we will devote much attention
to the practical application of the principles which have been described
in earlier chapters. To begin this assignment, we will examine the
contexts in which faith nurturing can occur. As we have already said,
the most effective nurturing will occur in a variety of settings where
faith can be appropriately explored. After considering the development
of these settings for the nurturing of faith, we will then deal with
specific programs or events for faith formation.

Create an Intentional Bias in Each Setting of Life

Every setting of our lives carries with it its own inherent bias.

The home, the school, the community, and the working environment are spaces filled with a particular bias (or slant or atmosphere). No environment or setting can be neutral. Even attempting to be neutral is a bias!

What we Christians must attempt to do is to carve out an "intentional" faith bias in several important life settings of young people. The intentional bias should be one that will be most facilitative to young persons as they shape their faith.

An intentional bias is one that we plan and develop which provides the most wholesome environment for faith development. A good teacher creates an intentional classroom bias. For example, if a teacher says, "In my classroom it is always appropriate to ask questions: tough questions, embarrassing questions, probing questions, doubting questions," such a statement reflects that teacher's intentional bias.

The Scripture verse "As for me and my house, we will serve the Lord" is a statement of intentional bias. If a coach says to her players, "Winning is important around here because that always motivates us to play our best. But our real purpose is to play hard, play fair, and play to learn the most from every situation, whether we're winning or losing," that statement reflects her intentional bias. The coach is deciding the atmosphere in which her teams will play the sport. If a family decides to make each Friday night a family night and further resolves that a time of prayer, singing, and Bible reading will occur three evenings a week around the dinner table, that would be providing an intentional bias toward the goal of faith nurturing.

It Is a New World for Youth

Youth today live in a new world in many ways. The settings in which the average teenager lives his or her life are often so conflicting and confusing that they leave youth drifting and rootless. No longer can we assume harmony even between the church and the home, or the home and the school, or the church and the youth peer group. A new approach to the faith nurturing needs of adolescents in this pluralistic era is needed. Let us first reflect upon a biblical passage.

In the creation story the Lord God said, "It is not good for the man to be alone. I will provide a partner for him" (Genesis 2:18, NEB). The Bible is telling us from the very beginning of our innate need for relatedness.

Nearly every person lives in a family—in a social context—within a set of primary relationships with other persons with whom we have constant contact and upon whom we mutually rely.

A revolution has been occurring within American society in regard to our understanding of the family. I believe the revolution can be identified by at least three changes in mentality.

1. The first change in mentality is typified by the way *we have broadened our ideas about the nuclear family.* Several decades ago, "family" meant a mom and dad and a daughter and a son and a dog named Spot.

Today more options are available; there are more choices of family life. My own family, being that of a couple, married for ten years, with no children, is today both accepted and acceptable. No longer are single adults looked upon as some strange breed of unsociables. Today single adults can live alone or with other adults, and in most circumstances the arrangement is both accepted and acceptable. The rise in divorce and marriage rates has caused both more single-parent families and more second marriages than ever before.

Consider all the living arrangements and options that are available today to senior adults: some live alone in their homes; some live in retirement villages or nursing homes; some move to the sun belt or to be near their children. Indeed, the revolution has changed our ideas of the nuclear family and what it means to live within a family.

2. There is a second aspect of the revolution. This relates to the human family—*the interdependency of all the peoples of the earth.* Ever since we first began looking at pictures of our earth as viewed from outer space as a tiny little glowing ball, we have become more convinced that we are on a spaceship called Earth. We are a global village—a world community—a common family, "humanitas." We have painfully learned that the price of oil is determined in a remote corner of the world by Arab oil ministers or the value of the dollar on European money markets. Even a strike by the city's garbage collectors reminds us of how much a family we really are—how interdependent we have become. Our idea of "world family" has unfolded.

3. A final aspect of the revolution in mentality regarding the family occurred within the church beginning in the late sixties and continuing on through the seventies. With this change in mentality we can no longer view the church as just an institution offering public

worship, opportunity for charity, and opportunity to teach children and youth. The church can be seen in a relational context, as a spiritual bond, a people, not an institution. *The church can be a quality of relationships among people with their God. It can be a family of the faithful.*

With these three changes in mentality, and with this revolution in our ideas of family, we have finally developed to the point where we can understand what the author of Ephesians meant when he wrote these words so long ago:

[Jesus] came and proclaimed the good news: peace to you who were far off, and peace to those who were near by; for through him we both alike have access to the Father. . . . You are *no longer aliens* in a foreign land, *but fellow-citizens* with God's people, *members of God's household.*

With this in mind, then, I kneel in prayer to the Father, from whom *every family* in heaven and on earth takes its name (Ephesians 2:17-19; 3:14-15, NEB, italics added).

What the author says is applicable to the primary family, the human family, and the church family.

With Deep Roots and Firm Foundations

We have described a revolution in regard to our concept of family life today, which closely parallels the three contexts of "family" as suggested by the author of Ephesians. The Scripture passage then moves in an interesting direction when it says, "With deep roots and firm foundations, may you be strong to grasp, with all God's people, . . . the love of Christ" (Ephesians 3:17-19, NEB).

The passage thus helps us to answer the question "How do we nurture youth and young adults in such a way that they will both claim and grow in the faith?" In other words, "How do people mature in the faith?" Ephesians stresses the utter importance of deep roots and firm foundations.

We need to expose our youth to loving families where faithfulness is as much a part of daily living as is sleeping or eating, to homes that both have faithful traditions and seek after a new depth of wisdom. *Youth need to be exposed to a loving church family* of faith where they are prized, where their contributions are valued, and where the stories of the faith are told and retold. *Youth need to be exposed to the world family* of God, where each person, of all varieties, regardless of culture, color, income, or class, is an important, precious, and worthy recipient of God's love.

Americans are becoming more and more a people who have no roots, no memory, and no heritage. They are becoming a people whose lives are so encircled by materialism and superficiality, so caught up and trapped by the present tense of selfish needs that many are losing their faith. They run from commitments. Their roots are eroding and not sinking down deep enough. Their foundations are cracking because they are not built upon a solid rock. Americans tend to be too cynical, too passive, and too hesitant.

And this is the kind of world in which young people must mature. The author of Ephesians implies that we must be nurtured with deep roots and firm foundations in the family, the church, and the world.

When we speak of adolescent faith development, we must talk of it inclusively, in a variety of settings. We must focus upon all settings, for roots will only be deep and foundations only secure if the faith of the young person is fed harmoniously and consistently by all the contexts and relationships in which his or her life is lived. There admittedly are some contexts where what we can do is very limited. But where influence can rightly be applied, let it be applied. The home, the church, the peer group, and the way we see and interact with the world are contexts in which we have a great influence.

The context in which we raise our children is of obvious impor-tance. If we raise our children with a heavy emphasis upon physical possessions and material security; and if we live in a suburb of look-alike, expensive houses and attend church on Sunday, participating and contributing meagerly; and if we live where children are only with people their age and adults their parents' age; where few societal structures or patterns or traditions are expected or practiced; where schools are highly secular arenas for competition in grades, sports, music, and the arts; then it is no wonder that our children are often marked by the superficiality of their spiritual commitment. Yet this is the very environment that many Americans are seeking.

Contrast this setting with an urban neighborhood heavily composed of Jews who wear traditional clothes, who walk with their families each sabbath to worship come rain or shine, who practice with regularity traditions of faith at the table, and who observe with great anticipation each holy season and celebration of the year. Here will be found young persons who will no doubt be steeped in spiritual resources.

Or think of the kind of setting provided by an active Protestant family attending an older city church with people of all ages, economic levels, and backgrounds; a church where exist long-time patterns of fellowship, sharing, personal support, and mission outreach. Families in this church choose to practice faith in their homes and cherish stories of faith. Parents participate and volunteer in the child's public school and teach in the church school, attend as a family an annual church retreat, and support actively a youth ministry in their church. A family is supported in times of crisis and in times of celebration by Christian friends and neighbors.

Another positive setting might be found in an inner-city black congregation in which the children sit through long worship services, yet experience real celebration; where children see their church sponsor housing and day care centers and assistance for those who could turn no other place. Morality is taught in the home and modeled by parents, even if not supported in tough neighborhood surroundings. Music is sung that communicates genuine feeling in a medium that youth appreciate; grandmothers sit in the same pew and care for grandchildren. The adolescent knows the same pastor that his parents had when they were his age.

Or think of a young person in a small church in a medium-sized city. The church is a family in a real sense. The size of the church allows persons of all ages to be known and prized. There are no narrow age groupings. The church is so small that nearly everything it does is intergenerational. Here a ten-year-old who loves to sing joins in the Sunday morning choir; the fifteen-year-old is in charge of preparing Communion; the five-year-old knows the pastor intimately. This is a church that relates easily and regularly to the members' homes.

Youth in these latter kinds of settings are the fortunate youth who have many spiritual resources with which to shape their faith.

A Difficult Setting: The Public School and Faith

In what settings should we exert influence toward mature faith nurturing? The Constitution of our country speaks forthrightly about the separation of church and state. It is clear that the public classroom is an inappropriate place for faith advocacy. Faith clarification can be done in the classroom, but we have already spoken of the disadvantage of completely divorcing the clarifying of faith from the advocating of faith. Clearly the public school is not the best setting for faith development. The gravity of this situation is recognized when we become aware of how much influence the public school has upon children and youth. When by law schools are forced to advocate neutrality in regard to faith, actually they are advocating a faith bias toward ''noninstitutional'' religion. They often espouse a belief in the doctrines of science, technology, and human knowledge, instead of religion.

While I wholeheartedly support the separation of church and state, and I agree that worship, prayers, or required devotional activity have no place in the public schools, I also realize how difficult it is to educate in a setting of such neutrality and how impossible it is to help persons in a holistic way.

Not only is faith advocation illegal in the public schools, but also as our society grows more and more complex and heterogenous, we will discover it to be increasingly difficult for teachers even to advocate particular values. In some communities it is difficult to speak of a value such as the two-parent family, the Puritan Work Ethic, patriotism, femininity or masculinity, humility as opposed to looking out for one's self, or the attitude of pushing to get what you want in life as opposed to turning the other cheek.

These are just a few of the challenges to face the public schools and the limited sphere of their influence. I am not questioning the value of public education, but I am stating a challenge the schools are facing in regard to areas of human concern they cannot legally or culturally affect. Sex education is perhaps one of the best examples of the problem. The schools are rightly teaching physiological and sexual information, but they must tread very softly as they deal with sexual morality. They can examine traditional moral arguments, but they are severely limited in the kind of active help youth desire as they ask: ''What's right? What's wrong? What's mature? What's appropriate?'' As society grows more complex and attitudes in homes, in culture, and in various religions toward sexuality become more diverse, the schools can do little more than stand on the diminishing common ground that remains.

Because the school has such a large influence with young persons today, even more pressure is placed on the other settings of their lives to fill in the gap.

Certainly the settings that offer themselves to faith development will vary from young person to young person and from situation to situation. *Generally, we can create an intentional bias for faith development in the home, in the church, and with the youth peer group.* Let us now examine how we can create a climate conducive to faith development in these three settings.

Faith Nurturing in the Home

The home is the "primary family." Its influence is pervasive on all aspects of the young person's maturation. All parents, consciously or unconsciously, establish an atmosphere in their families, marriages, and homes that affects all areas of the young person's development.

If parents are not intentional in passing along the faith foundation of their lives, then the possibility surely exists that they will unconsciously pass along a lesser faith. Only by their intentionally deciding upon the practice of faith traditions and upon a pattern of faithfulness in the home will the best impact of their faith be felt. Young parents need to be trained and helped as they face this responsibility. Many adults come back into the church when they begin to have children because they want to nurture them in this environment. Their return often also means a renewed commitment to their own spiritual journey.

Homes can and should be places for traditions of nearness and directness. All four types of Faith-Shaping Memories can be provided at home: headline experiences, repetition experiences, personally touching events, and significant relationships.

I remember several occasions for directness in my childhood home. None I remember so well as the conversations with my father around the time of my baptism. It was a time of significant sharing. We tried and failed and tried again to have family devotions daily in our home. The repetition and pattern of nearness were important, as was the struggle to accomplish it.

The significant relationships with other Christian adults who came frequently into our home when I was a child continue to nourish and sustain me to this day. I remember the personally touching event when my sister and I gave, as an anniversary present, a wood-carved podium upon which our family Bible was placed.

Faith should be uplifted and celebrated in the home. We should not be reluctant or feel unqualified to do so. Sacred celebrations of new births, baptisms, decisions, changes, graduations, completions, beginnings can all be held. Gratitude for the gift of daily life and the bountiful gifts God has given us can be constantly felt and expressed.

A home should be a place where Christian friends and a Christian support community gathers. Youth should feel included in all of this. Pastors and other important persons of faith should be seen in the home. Symbols of faith can be prominently displayed. Sharing times, family nights, daily devotions, meal prayers, late-night discussions, families attending church together as a unit: all these and more can shape the intentional faith bias that parents hope to provide.

One of the most classic problems in the home is found where the parents were brought up in a strict moral and spiritual environment in their childhood and adolescent years. But the parents received an education and in the process outgrew their faith traditions, becoming more freethinking and open-minded. They raised their children with an emphasis on choices rather than commitments. There were only casual requirements made of their children in relation to the faith. Today, the parents still have their own commitments, molded in their earlier years, but they failed to transmit them. Now the parents' faith tradition means little or nothing to the children.

These parents emphasize choices over commitments. A balance between the two is difficult, and it seems far more desirable to err on the side of commitments than of choices. The child can always rebel as the parents did. I know many parents who so value choices for their children and are so embarrassed to emphasize commitments that their children grow up without commitments. The parents are highly committed, faithful people, but it was not the emphasis of their child rearing to pass along this commitment.

Every parent, at a minimum, ought annually to tell the story of their faith to their maturing children at the level of the children's maturity and readiness.

Many parents I have known have been extremely concerned that their children have every opportunity afforded to them. For this reason success in school is very often the most important parental value. They also want to see their children excel in music, art, dance, drama, or sports, and so these activities often consume an enormous amount of time. These and other priorities can squeeze opportunity for faith nurturing into a small corner. I have no doubt that all of these activities are important and wholesome. But if we concentrate on building the frame and structure of the lives of our children while ignoring the foundation, the building will eventually crumble. We produce talented and educated young adults who have no roots, no deep convictions, no sound ambitions that will give their life purpose and meaning.

Many college students who have been given every material thing and every opportunity for good schooling and an active training in areas of personal interest but have not been rooted in mature faith find that they are not happy, nor do they find success in the most wholesome sense of that word.

Faith Nurturing in the Church

Some churches do excel in creating an atmosphere conducive to faith development, but many other churches do not seem to understand faith development or know how to nurture faith in children, youth, or adults.

Churches need to wrestle with these fundamental questions:

—Do we want church membership for youth with casual reference to Christian discipleship?

—Or do we want Christian discipleship with its implied claim of church membership?

Very often churches can handle the tangible nature of the first question and not the intangible quality of the latter. For matters of ease and security, churches often opt for an emphasis upon membership needs of the institutional church, while neglecting to instill authentic Christian discipleship within young people.

The church too often today has focused upon the "frills" of religion and not on the essential ingredient of faith. Many churches seem confused and have a blurred sense of their own identity and mission. Often the emphasis has been placed on maintenance functions of the institution rather than on faith formation and inspiration. Many churches today are seeking to revitalize themselves by becoming more aware of their reason for being, their purpose, their identity, and their special calling from God. As churches gain a clearer sense of their mission, they will surely realize the importance of faith as the cornerstone of the church's life. They will realize how important it is to surround children and youth with a community that lives through faithful traditions and whose members share an intimate experience of love and grace. The people will experience the church on mission with one another and in the wider world.

As a local church is clear about its theology and mission, it will be more able to nurture young persons in the faith and to model before them, week in and week out, which values and beliefs and ideals are worth a lifetime of commitment.

As we think about youth involvement in the church, we must recognize that young persons generally do not relate directly to their church by their own free choice. Regardless of confirmation or baptism, their church commitment is generally made through their parents who first chose for themselves a certain expression of faith and selected a church based upon that expression. Consequently, the person's attitude and commitment toward a church are usually heavily influenced by the attitude and commitment of the parents.

A parent who is intimately involved in the fellowship of a church and who cares deeply about his or her community of faith will more naturally open doors to his or her children to follow that example. A parent who pays dues to the church, worships casually, and participates in leadership only when made to feel guilty will influence his or her children along these lines.

Thus, our ability to influence youth in the church is heavily influenced by the commitments of the parents. Parents who think they can "send Johnny to church" to get the faith, while staying away themselves, are sadly mistaken because the church faces a nearly impossible task.

The church family should be a special community where youth feel accepted, prized, and needed. It should be a place for friends. It cannot be so formal or so "adult" or so dignified that it pushes youth off into a corner. The church should be a place where intergenerational relationships grow and mature. It should be a place where youth do not have to do anything or perform anything to be accepted. The spontaneous adult-youth relationships that can unfold in a church are often the most determinative upon faith shaping.

A church cannot completely delegate faith development of children and youth to specialized age level ministries. In such a case youth would never see any example of faith except that of their peers. *Youth can never find a place within the traditions and stories and values of a community of faith if they are kept on its periphery.* The church must offer itself, its whole self, as a creative and secure place for personal growth for children, for youth, and for adults. Adolescents who experience their parents, their pastors, their advisers, and their friends growing in the faith as a result of their church experience will more likely follow their example.

Faith Nurturing with Adolescent Peers

The peer age group is perhaps where churches have traditionally focused most of their attention and developed the best resources for faith nurturing. It is a strategically important setting for developing patterns of nearness and directness. It is a pivotal setting for providing faith-shaping memories. Many church-sponsored youth groups plan headline experiences for youth, such as youth mission trips, musicals, camps, or retreats. They provide repetition experiences through group traditions and practices passed along throughout the six years of junior high and senior high. They provide personally touching events and significant relationships. There is a great deal to be affirmed in the church's youth peer ministry.

One of the most important factors in faith development with an adolescent peer group is the adult sponsor. These dedicated persons can be very influential models. They can be advocates and clarifiers of faith. They can guide youth as they work their way through one Faith-Shaping Task after another. *The adult sponsor is one of the first and few adults with whom a young person can form a deep relationship, who is not in a position of hierarchy over the youth, as contrasted with teachers and parents.* A relationship of equality and friendship makes a tremendous impression. Adult workers with senior high youth and with young adults should be trained in developing relationships that share authority and collegiality with youth.

The church peer community is often a collection of adolescents who do not see one another except at church and who might not share common interests. They perhaps would not "choose" to be friends if it were not for the common church relationship. The pluralism in this situation and the diverse personalities and interests that are represented make this an exceptional opportunity for tolerance, patience, growth, and compassion. It is one of the few settings where the average teenager relates to his or her peers on the basis of such pluralism.

Peer ministries should be fun, active, recreational, and missional.

They also need to be centered upon personal sharing, worship, prayer, reflection, and faith formation. The balance should be held. One should never use these groups to press or push faith, but neither should one be embarrassed or reluctant to center these groups upon faith-filled endeavors. They can present the faith both nearly and directly.

In my experience I have found that when parents and the church's leadership truly support adolescent peer ministries, these are truly effective agents for faith development. They exert a subtle yet significant influence upon many young people even though the time investment is small as compared to other settings of their lives.

These peer ministries are one of the few places where faith can be shown to intersect the popular youth culture that young persons experience in other settings. The church has been correct in placing emphasis upon peer groups. If we had been exerting an equal emphasis upon the faith potential of the church as a whole and upon the home, we would be much more effective faith agents.

Flexibility in Faith Nurturing in the Church

Churches need to develop several "tracks" for their involvement with youth. We cannot single-mindedly or rigidly expect all young persons to be attracted to all phases of a local church's programming any more than we expect all adults to respond to all programs offered them. Smaller churches, fortunately, need fewer tracks than larger ones because they can be more personal within their church family.

Youth mature through various stages in relationship with their community of faith. We need to respond to these stages sensitively.

For example, in my church there are five programming tracks available for youth. We have church school classes, a youth fellowship group designed on a retreat model, an annual discipleship emphasis, three choirs (bell choirs and vocal), and the participation of youth in the church family (worship, teaching children's classes, financial support, leadership in decision-making groups, intergenerational relationships, church dinners, fellowship events, etc.).

We have several youth who follow their parents' example and participate only on Sunday mornings in worship and church school. Others are primarily interested in music and limit their participation to the choirs. Others participate in other tracks.

As a congregation, we have a tremendous impact with those youth who participate actively in all tracks available to them. Usually, though not always, their parents are strong advocates of faith.

As their pastor, it is my prayer and hope that all youth (as well as persons of all ages) become more involved in their family of faith. I believe that hope is solidly based upon a biblical mandate. But I also realize that not every programming track will match the needs of all young people. It is OK for some to opt in and out of various groups as they mature and change, as long as there is some sense of mutual accountability to it.

The task of the church is to engage youth in significant ways. We need a variety of offerings to do this. We need to be freed from the numbers game and from competition between different programs. We need to recognize that young people and their spiritual development have the priority. The so-called "success" of our programs should always be a second consideration.

I would suggest these guidelines:

1. We should never ask or expect more from youth than we are asking of ourselves as adults.

2. The door to participation needs always to be open, and an invitation actually and occasionally given to each young person. All youth need to feel a warm encouragement to be involved in the life of their church.

3. We need to believe that it's OK for youth to participate at various levels, and we need not induce guilt within them for lack of full involvement.

4. Parents and leaders should expect involvement from youth. For younger youth the adult role is more definite and authoritative. For older youth accountability needs to exist, though more choices and personal space can now be introduced. For older adolescents and young adults in the Faith-Shaping Task of Separating, freedom should be granted regarding their faith commitment and their participation. These youth still need to know that we care and that we think faith is of ultimate importance, but the accountability now takes on an entirely new shape. It is now open to full negotiation and mutuality.

5. Avoid competition among various programs and among their supporters and leaders within the church. Harmonize and blend; co-operate and communicate. Affirm all leaders privately and publicly. All leaders need to be aware of the unique value of each programming

track and how it fits into the total ministry. Develop an effective system of communication and coordination.

6. The discipleship potential of each programming track needs to be realized. If a particular track has none, then its value is questionable. Some programs by necessity communicate discipleship more subtly, but they can still be just as essential.

7. Involve youth in decision making and in leadership regarding those areas that affect them in the life of the church. Make them full partners in these ministries.

8. Never allow youth programming to be seen as "one small concern of the church." Do not push it into a closet! Build congregation-wide support and involvement with the youth and with programs affecting them.

Faith Nurturing Through a Global Perspective

The church is one of the few international or global organizations to which youth can belong. Often they are aware of the church's mission with various ethnic groups within our own nation and with various cultures and economic levels around the world. Today, more and more they are taught to appreciate and respect the diversity of God's created world. They are learning of the give-and-take of Christian mission, the up and down, the in and out, the back and forth among language groups, races, nationalities, and continents, all in the name of Christ.

Adolescents in such enlightened communities of faith gain a unique world view. They understand the world in more sensitive, involved, and connectional ways than a school geography class could ever provide. They understand that a young person in Zaire can stand in relation to the very same God and express faith within a different culture, with different symbols and meanings. They can feel "at one" with people of different ages and colors.

The church is a unique setting that we provide for faith development. The world is no longer totally "out there" or hostile. Young persons in the church know that they are citizens of the world and citizens of God's kingdom on earth.

Chapter 8

Practices
and
Proposals

The best "program" includes adults who at once prize their faith, care deeply about youth, and who, with great sincerity and some ability to communicate, mutually explore faith with youth in natural and frequent ways.

DISCIPLESHIP EDUCATION: that which helps persons who are seeking or continuing in Christian discipleship to make the necessary decisions and actions appropriate to their faith development

In this chapter will be listed a "sampling" of specific programs or events that can nurture faith.

Several of the ideas can be implemented on a regional or associational basis, and others can be used in the context of the local church as it develops its own program.

We must recognize that there is no ultimate program to nurture youth in the faith! *The best "program" includes adults who at once prize their faith, care deeply about youth, and who, with great sincerity and some ability to communicate, mutually explore faith with youth in natural and frequent ways.*

As soon as we understand that guiding principle, we have assimilated a great bit of wisdom. Persons who attend workshops or seminary aren't necessarily better than those who do not. Well-read persons don't necessarily transmit faith better than those who are not well read.

However, the nurturing of faith obviously depends upon programming. What is offered here are suggestions as a springboard to your own creativity.

Some Nearness Proposals

Nearness has to do with how close you have been in your upbringing to the traditions of faithfulness.

Nearness dictates that we not wait until the child is in the sixth or seventh grade with our concerns of nurturing faith. Nearness to the faith begins when parents first decide to have children. If the parents learn early how to nurture faith in their home and how to encourage it through the church, much of the victory is already won.

Therefore, it is legitimate that one component of faith development with youth emphasizes first-time parents or parents with very young children.

"Sharing the Story"

"Sharing the Story of Faith with Your Children" is a one-day workshop that can be offered by regions, associations, or a coalition of local churches for expectant parents or parents of young children. The program is deliberately focused on ways of nurturing faith in the home and through the church.

A curricular package could be developed using trained professional leaders. A great deal of research and thought should go into the development of a high quality event that would be worth generating enthusiasm and ownership among young parents. Parents could be led to examine their own unique responsibilities and shown ways to choose and begin their own faith traditions in the home. The home, as a context for faith nurturing, would be the central thrust of the worship.

Parental Faith Nurturing Classes

Churches could use the information in this book, as well as from other sources, to begin teaching parents of junior high and senior high youth the role of faith nurturing in the home and in their family's priorities. A church school elective series or an evening series would be a suitable setting. Parents might respond favorably to such an offering since many are confused, fearful, or uncertain about this subject and are seeking help. This book has been written for parents and nurturers as well as for other leaders in the church.

Faith Memory Journals

Bibles are given to third grade children in many Protestant churches. Within the Bible are the memories of faith of the Christian community. Also in early elementary years we should consider beginning a Faith Memory Journal for each child.

A Faith Memory Journal is a loose-leaf binder which is kept in a secure place at the church. On the pages of this Faith Memory Journal would be recorded observations, experiences, questions, ideas, and thoughts of that particular young person.

Church school teachers would be asked to journalize for each student each year. Parents, also, would be invited to journalize, as would pastors, and any others in close contact. Pages from the binder would be distributed to these persons or could be requested by these persons.

As the children mature into youth, they, too, would be given pages during a church school class from time to time, such as the conclusion of retreats, before baptism or first Communion, or at the end of thinking through a personal problem, etc.

The Journal would not be inclusive of all the shaping memories and experiences that have nurtured that person in the faith. But it would be indicative of reactions of persons significant to the youth as well as the youth's own reactions to experiences. It would give an overview of the nurturing that person has experienced. It would be a "report card" in the most wholesome sense of that word.

One volunteer in the church would coordinate and keep these Faith Memory Journals current and, therefore, useful. No one could take the notebook out of the room in which it is kept. While the Journal is not secret, neither is it for public inspection. It is kept for the sole purpose of being helpful to the young person in remaining nearer to his or her faith tradition.

The Journals would remain under the supervision of the church until high school graduation, when they would be presented as gifts to the graduates. The Journals might have a large impact over the coming decade as these young adults face a variety of changes and challenges in their lives.

During their youth years, the young people could look, with supervision, at the Journal at any time of their choosing. During the first three months of junior high, the first three months of senior high, and the last three months of high school, the pastor or other resourceful lay leader would meet with each young person for the purpose of examining the Journal and discussing its implications. These times would, no doubt, have tremendous appeal to the youth, as all of us like to see something written about our lives. The review would also provide the adult with a specific and focused time to discuss concerns of faith with each young person.

The sole purpose of the Journal is to collect some of the faith experiences and thoughts of that person to help the person in the attempt to synthesize and choose his or her own faith stance.

Admittedly, a Faith Memory Journal program would be a significant undertaking. A great deal of administrative procedure would have to be established. But the work involved is really no greater than the record-keeping system we administer in most of our Sunday church schools, and the Journal could be far more beneficial than counting heads on Sunday morning.

If some churches find themselves pressed for volunteer help, perhaps they should take a long look at some of their volunteer jobs and "reprioritize" them. The Journals should be no more difficult for small churches than large churches.

Here is how a church might establish the Faith Memory Journal for its children and youth.

JUDSON CHURCH: FAITH MEMORY JOURNAL

1. In the formal worship service on the first Sunday of the fall children entering the third grade will be given a Bible by the church and will be presented with their Faith Memory Journal. The Journal will be a three-ring notebook with lined pages. The children will keep their Bibles and "deposit" their Journals in a special closet or cabinet at the church. A service of dedication will be held on this Sunday.

2. The pastors and/or a trained lay leader will sit down with each youth to examine the Journal at the following times: (*a*) the time preceding baptism or confirmation; (*b*) during the first three months of junior high; (*c*) during the first three months of senior high; (*d*) during the last three months of senior high; and (*e*) other times arranged by individual request. These five times would be occasions for reflection, counseling, guidance, and examination of the Journal by the adult and youth together.

3. Input into the Journal will be made by the following persons at the following times (in all cases a page from the book will be distributed rather than the entire book):

   - Each March an "Input Sheet" would be mailed to the parents. When returned, it would be included in the Journal.
   - Youth fellowship group sponsors would be asked each April to journalize in each book.
   - Church school teachers of grades 3-12 would be invited each May to journalize in each student's book.
   - Pastors would be invited to make an entry in each Journal in June.
   - In September, both church school teachers of youth and youth fellowship advisers would each be asked to select a time when the young persons themselves would make an entry in their own Journal. If desired, youth can make entries in one another's Journal.
   - In October, a general notice would be given to the congregation so that members can request an input form for a Journal.

4. A director of the Faith Memory Journals will be appointed for a three-year term for the following tasks:

   - to keep the Journals in safe and secure surroundings
   - to mail out entry forms according to the above schedule
   - to place completed forms into the appropriate Journal
   - to prepare new Journals for children entering the church or to those entering third grade and to present the Journals to graduating seniors.

5. A Sample "Faith Memory Journal Input Sheet"
   This sheet will be placed, when completed, into the Faith Memory Journal of _____, _____.
   (name)   (age)

Please return this sheet to the Director of the Faith Memory Journals by _____ so that it might be placed in the permanent record.
            (date)

—On this sheet please record an experience you have shared or an observation you have made that has shown a growing awareness by this person of his or her own faith, an understanding of himself or herself, or a maturity in relation to his or her values, beliefs, or goals.

—For youth recording on their own sheets, please record what your faith means to you now or any experience you have had that has deepened your faith in God. Be specific!

Directness Proposal

Directness has to do with how the faith is actually presented to youth.

Directness happens most effectively in natural situations where adults who care take the time to share and discuss with young persons struggling with their own faith questions.

The Directness proposal presented here is needed because adults have such trouble presenting the faith directly to youth. We often either overdo it (we push and shove them) or we underdo it (we're embarrassed to bring it up).

There are several concentrated times in the development of adolescents in our culture that are pivotal. Those times which are most universal and easiest to identify are the first three months of junior high, the first three months of senior high, and the sixteenth and eighteenth birthdays.

These are times when youth enter into a new stage of expectations. More things are expected of a junior high student than of one still in elementary school. Expectations are thrust upon them not only by teachers, parents, and other adults, but also by other youth their own age. The same is true of the entry into the world of high school. Different behavior and mentality are expected. As young persons face the time to drive, society grants youth a new expectation. They are given more freedom and their mobility increases dramatically. With "wheels" they can have many more choices. In our society, we have recognized the eighteenth birthday as an entry into adult responsibilities. Freedom to buy liquor and to exercise the vote are but two common indications. Youth who cross this point in life are very aware of this change. And, finally, graduation from high school nearly always brings to the surface the heavy burden of more personal independence, painfully lonely decisions, and a moving out to a new frontier. Most high school seniors are quite open to new possibilities during this time.

At each of these points, youth enter what amounts to a new world. To meet this new world head-on, a great amount of "quick" maturation is often required. Some of the maturation is positive, and some of it is negative. Regardless, these are potent times to intrude! They are strategic times to make an impact by encouraging youth to ask: "What does faith mean? What potential does it hold for me now?"

The Directness proposal, then, is a *Third-Month Retreat,* a weekend retreat sponsored by an association, an area, or a consortium of churches for youth during the third month of junior high, the third month of senior high, and/or the third from the last month of senior high. The emphasis would be on the directness of the faith at that point of development.

A standard curricular format could be developed and used by skilled and trained personnel in these settings. The context of each retreat would need to be tailored to the unique needs of each age setting.

For example, the junior high retreat could emphasize the beginnings of faith questions; the first senior high retreat could emphasize faith shaping; and the graduation retreat could emphasize life directions and the faith.

A New Strategy for Discipleship Education (Nearness and Directness)

Whenever we speak of the acquisition of faith or of forming a deeper relationship with God, we are speaking of discipleship, and efforts toward these aims are called discipleship education.

Discipleship education is an orphan child in the church. In most churches the structure is such that no one governing board takes responsibility for it. In the traditional structure it falls between the board of deacons with its mandate for spiritual vitality and the board of Christian education with its mandate to educate within the church. Consequently, no one really takes responsibility for discipleship education. Proof of this is the common habit of "assigning" all such efforts to the pastor. Discipleship classes in many churches are even called "the pastor's class." Baptismal preparation is usually the pastor's responsibility. The lay responsibility is reduced to assistance in the dressing rooms.

The same is true for most denominational program agencies. There are few ongoing thrusts in these agencies for discipleship education.

There is a tremendous narrowness in our mentality toward discipleship education. Our minds immediately race to the junior high age and a discipleship class in which we present the faith and gain the youth's response to it. We think of the baptism or confirmation that will follow, and then we are "done" with it until the next year and another class of junior highs.

There is nothing wrong in and of itself with this approach. However, very few of us would say that discipleship ends with a first-time decision. In fact, most of us would say that it is only the beginning. We would affirm that being a Christian disciple is a lifelong process— a journey where change, growth, and maturity are constant factors.

And, finally, few churches plan a congregation-wide strategy for discipleship education or faith formation. Without such a strategy we leave to chance what should be entrusted to our most purposeful and thoughtful planning. We should not treat discipleship education in a hit-or-miss manner. *Every church needs a comprehensive and harmonious plan for discipleship education for every age group.* Small churches and large churches alike should be equally able to accomplish this.

We can no longer have a restricted view of discipleship education. Discipleship education has to do with the faith development of us all, regardless of our stage of maturity.

Preparation for discipleship is the work of the entire church and is an ongoing, lifelong responsibility.

For too long, only perfunctory attention has been given to the training of new members. Little or no concern has been directed to an ongoing process of preparation and development of all members. The price of this neglect is a low level of commitment, a limited measure of involvement, and a general degree of ineffectiveness. . . . There is a growing feeling among many leaders that preparation for discipleship must involve a more significant and demanding and comprehensive set of experiences. The formal step of identifying with the church as a member is primary and basic. At the same time, this particular act must be kept in perspective in order that persons may continue to grow in their discovery of the fullest dimensions of the function of a disciple of Jesus Christ. If we accept the fact that discipleship is an ongoing process and is a lifelong experience, then it will be necessary to expand our concepts and practices with respect to discipleship preparation.[1]

Discipleship education is that which helps persons who are seeking or continuing in Christian discipleship to make necessary decisions and actions leading to appropriate faith development. From this definition, we can see that discipleship education clearly deals with the personal decisions and directions of the disciple's life. In this type of education we are intending to help persons take the necessary "next steps" of their faith development. For youth, discipleship education is an effort to help them as they work through the tasks of shaping faith.

Because discipleship education is one of the church's most important tasks, *we need to develop specific strategies to accomplish our broad goal of discipleship education.* These strategies should be built into a master plan involving the total membership of a church. Every person, young and old, who is a part of the church, should have the opportunity to share in a well-designed training experience for his or her role as a disciple in a community of believers and one's role as a witness of love in the larger community.

Thus, the following points form the central thrust of the master plan:

1. Discipleship education concerns itself with the advancement of a person's faith development.

2. Discipleship education addresses itself to each person, regardless of maturity.

3. There will need to be a different emphasis with children, junior high youth, senior high youth, adults, new members, and newly baptized believers in regard to discipleship education.

4. Discipleship education is *not* just for the new Christian, nor is it just for junior high youth.

5. One of the prime objectives of the church school is discipleship education. Whatever else is planned or accomplished should balance and augment weekly Sunday study.

[1] Grant Hanson, "Introduction: Preparation for Discipleship," *Baptist Leader,* vol. 35, no. 10 (January, 1974), p. 2. Used by permission of American Baptist Board of Education and Publication.

6. Theologically, items of highest priority for a meaningful experience seem to be:

a. to assume that all discipleship efforts relate each disciple to the larger community of faith and that such efforts not be kept in "one closet of the church."

b. to instill an understanding of discipleship as a lifelong journey not limited to one program or class, nor limited only to baptism or confirmation.

c. to cast discipleship as an active, interesting, and provocative endeavor that helps a person focus the growth of his or her personal faith.

A MODEL DISCIPLESHIP MASTER PLAN FOR A LOCAL CHURCH
A Discipleship Plan for Children
Infant Dedication or Baptism

IN THE CHURCH: The formal dedication or baptism as an act of worship before the church family.

IN THE HOME: A home dedication surrounding the birth of a new baby and preceding the public service at church. A home dedication further stimulates the parents and the close support community of that family to take seriously their responsibility as interpreters of faith. This home dedication could be done by the pastor in the home with a small group of invited guests. The intent would be to personalize the church's ministry to the family on the occasion of the birth of each child.

Bibles to the Third Graders

The gift of modern translations of the Bible to each incoming third grader is an act of discipleship.

Faith Memory Journals to Third Graders

In an act of public worship the third graders would be shown their own Faith Memory Journals. The Journals would be dedicated with public prayer and then placed in safekeeping with the other Journals. Throughout the child's experiences within the church the Journal would be continuously updated.

Children's Participation

By involving children as essential parts of the overall fabric of the church, we are conducting an essential discipleship emphasis. Children need to experience the church as an intergenerational loving community. In addition, children need to participate actively and regularly in age level church programs such as vacation Bible school, church school, choirs, and other special events as an important part of discipleship nurturing.

A Discipleship Plan for Youth
The Christian Discipleship Journey for Junior High Youth

The Christian Discipleship Journey is a five-week annual endeavor for junior highs.

It presents discipleship as a lifelong journey and sees this junior high journey as merely one segment along the way. The journey is intergenerational in that it combines one adult partner (another junior high's parent) with each young person. It is an individual journey with points for cooperation and for group participation. It teaches the youth how to covenant to accomplish a personal goal. The Journey is highly structured, though it has many options.

In the Journey are four Destinations. Each year the youth select one of these Destinations to explore: Bible and Belief, Church Heritage, Serving and Caring, and the Local Church. In the three years of junior high each young person will have completed three of the four Destinations.

A complete description of the expectations for each Destination would be prepared and distributed to the teams at the beginning of each year. (See the Appendix for an example of how one church structured this Discipleship Journey for junior high youth.)

The completion of each year's Journey is recognized in front of the church by the presentation of a certificate. Junior high youth participate annually in the Journey regardless of baptism or confirmation decisions.

ROAD MAP FOR THE CHRISTIAN DISCIPLESHIP JOURNEY

1. One parent (or substitute) accompanies each young person in the Journey.

2. Each young person is teamed with one parent (not her or his own), and these teams are partners for the Journey to share together in the experience.

3. Each adult-youth team "covenants" to arrive at one of the Destinations of the Journey.

4. For each Destination there will be some required and some optional projects. The projects must be the work of the youth, but the adults are to be supportive in the completion of each project.

OVERALL REQUIREMENTS FOR ALL JOURNEYERS

1. Attend one session with the minister without one's parents. This is a concept-building session on the discipleship concepts of "belonging" and "believing."

2. Because discipleship also includes fun relationships between people, each participant will join in a fellowship event.

3. Create a sharing display which will be viewed by the congregation on the concluding Sunday of this year's Journey. The display will share with the church the area in which you have explored.

Faith Memory Journal Sessions

During the first three months of junior high, the time preceding baptism or confirmation, the first three months of senior high, the last three months of senior high, and at other times as requested, young persons will meet individually with the pastor or trained lay leader to examine their own Journals and their spiritual growth.

Third-Month Retreats

Retreats for consideration of faith could be offered by a consortium of churches to youth in the third month of junior high and/or the third month of senior high and/or the third from the last month of senior high.

Senior High Christian Discipleship Weekend Retreat

The potential value in getting away for a twenty-four-hour retreat to explore discipleship with senior high youth is real. This time provides a more secure and relaxed environment in which youth can truly grapple with their own faith development. "Where am I in the faith?" and "Where am I with the faith?" are key questions. Each senior high youth selects one adult in the church (not one's parent) to ask to be his or her partner on the retreat. The presence of one adult for each youth ensures that the youth will take the experience more seriously.

Senior High Mission Trip

A senior high mission involvement trip is a good discipleship effort because with proper orientation and preparation, it is an opportunity to put faith into action and to experience a broader "sample" of life. It can be an eye-opening and deepening experience.

Youth Participation

Youth need to be accepted as full participants in the life of the church. This is an important ingredient in their own faith development. They need to experience the church not only as a loving community but also as a community that accepts them and empowers them.

In addition to these specific programs, regular and active participation in youth fellowship groups, choirs, church school classes, summer camping programs, and other special events are pivotal elements in discipleship nurturing.

A Discipleship Plan for Adults

Discipleship for adults is of critical importance because it is crucial for an adult disciple to keep growing in faith throughout his or her life. For example, it can be a matter of discipleship when someone goes through a career evaluation, or a question of parenting, or a problem in a marriage, or a period of loneliness or despair. If adults are not able in any of these situations to ask the question "What would God have me do?" or "In what direction does my faith lead me?" then they have lost the cutting edge of what it means to be a disciple.

Discipleship education for adults is using faith as the vehicle for personal growth. Whenever the resources of faith are brought to bear in a "teachable moment," that is the time when discipleship education occurs.

The challenge with adults is to find a model that is appealing, will truly get to the heart of the matter, but is not threatening. Unlike children and youth who have been traditionally expected to respond to discipleship education efforts, adults do not expect this of themselves. Beyond the few who participate in adult church school, the church's faith development efforts with adults have been sadly lacking. Unless the faith of adults is growing and deepening, it will be difficult for them or the church to motivate the faith of young people.

The Greek Discipleship System for Adults

Using Greek words from the New Testament, we will consider five different approaches to discipleship education that can be sponsored by a church as the need arises. No adult would be expected to participate in all programs. But all adults would be encouraged to become involved in those things that meet their own individual needs.

KOINONIA (pronounced "coy-no-*nee*-ah"): Koinonia means fellowship, and this group would meet for nine to twelve weeks in midwinter and Lent to build Christian community and fellowship. These persons would divide their energy into study, prayer, worship, small group sharing, mission service projects, and recreational fellowship. They would meet in homes and eat together. They would share leadership after one person or couple acts as conveners.

CHARIS (pronounced "*care*-iss"): Charis means grace, and this group would meet for nine to twelve months on a contractual basis to experience God's grace and to discover one's own personal gifts and resources in a secure environment. Groups would contract together to maintain group discipline. A trained leader would be secured.

AGAPE (pronounced "uh-*gah*-pay"): Agape means sacrificial love. The agape meal, the Lord's Supper, would be celebrated in a simple, intimate worship experience held on Wednesday nights for eight weeks each fall. The service would be comprised of a time for hymn singing without accompaniment, a time for sharing of personal and congregational concerns, a time for group prayer, a time for biblical reflection and response, and a time for the Lord's Supper in closing. Persons would be recruited to bake bread and to share in the biblical reflection. Communion could be received in unique and innovative ways to symbolize the scriptural lesson of the evening.

METANOIA (pronounced "met-ta-*noy*-ya"): Metanoia means to change one's way of being. A Friday evening through Saturday afternoon format would be followed in this once-a-year event. The focus of this time would be to identify and begin to attain new areas of personal and faith growth. It might begin by encouraging participants to inventory their life and faith for self-evaluation. Then, encourage persons to determine their own personal agenda from the choices that confront them. A group and individual process could then be developed through which the adult disciples identify the next step of their Christian journey. Finally, the retreat would close with a celebration of discipleship. Child care would be provided.

THE LAOS (pronounced "*lay*-ahs") FELLOWSHIP: Laos means the people of God. This group would meet the first Friday of each month in the home(s) of its sponsors. Participants could be prospects, new members, or those members seeking to become more deeply involved in the life of the church; they would be encouraged to attend six consecutive sessions. Curriculum for the six sessions would attempt to build deeper relationships with the church, provide handles for increased involvement, and communicate information on the church, its beliefs, heritage, and style.

Sharing the Story

First-time parents would attend a regional conference to help them to be trained in the task of building a strong faith foundation within their home.

Faith-Nurturing Classes

These classes would be held on occasion for parents of youth and older children to train them in the faith development process of adolescents.

Use of Church Covenants

Churches whose heritage it is to use covenants have a tremendous reservoir of potential for faith development. If covenants are taken seriously and are written in such a way as to encourage implementation of their vows, then their use will have many ramifications upon personal and corporate faithfulness. The church can renew its covenant each year, perhaps on Pentecost, as a time of recommitment and renewal.

Adult Participation

Adult discipleship can be fostered by intentional and reflective participation by adults in worship, study, fellowship, mission, leadership, and stewardship within the life of the faith community.

A Discipleship Plan for First-Time Decisions
Prebaptism Counseling or Class

The class provides an opportunity to determine if a candidate is aware of the magnitude of the decision and to explore all facets of discipleship to Christ.

Baptism (or Confirmation)

Performance of the ordinance is an act of discipleship. A personal celebration should follow each baptism. Whether this is a dinner hosted by deacons of the church or a party planned by a supportive group of friends and supporters, no baptism should be "uncelebrated"! Youth will be individually contacted each spring to determine their readiness for baptism.

Hand of Fellowship and First Communion

The Hand of Fellowship symbolizes a person joining the church and is an act of discipleship. The first Communion can be highlighted by a special litany or by sitting at the Communion table with the church leaders.

Faith Partners

Persons should not be baptized and forgotten. A deacon or person appointed by the deacons will be assigned to each new convert for the purpose of being a partner and a supporter during this crucial initial time. The partners can meet at three- and six-month intervals after baptism to take an inventory of the person's faith progress. The purpose of the dialogue and the relationship would be to express interest, support, and concern.

Chapter 9

A Person of Christian Faith

The front side and the back side of the gospel—a free and accountable love—are what it means to be a person of Christian faith today. Young people who begin to grasp this gospel are well on their way to mature faith and fullness of life.

Much of what has been said about the faith nurturing of youth would be applicable to the nurture of any faith, Christian or otherwise, particularly in a pluralistic culture like ours. Young persons growing up in a Buddhist home need faith clarifiers and advocates; they need practices of nearness and directness; they will pass through the same faith-shaping tasks. Faith nurturing of youth is a universal task of all religions.

We, however, want to concern ourselves with the sharing of Christian faith with youth. The quality of faith that young people experience is greatly (though not entirely) influenced by what we as adults and parents extend to them. In a special sense each denomination or church, as a faithful community, must decide for itself what is important to pass along.

This chapter will sketch out the broadest directions in which mature Christian faith travels without attempting to split theological or doctrinal hairs. In the Christian church there is a variety of beliefs, stances, and doctrines. Much of that variety is faithful to Christian experience and to the Scriptures. Much of it stems from a difference in emphasis rather than substance. The variety is one of the things that makes Christianity so universal, creative, and exciting.

What You Believe Matters!

There is in American culture today a nonchalance about faith. There is an "anything goes" mentality. Many people believe that "it doesn't matter what you believe, just as long as you believe in something." "Something" too often means "anything," and "anything" too often means "nothing." Some of this mentality reflects a tolerance of the plurality of faiths that we see exhibited in modern, urban America today. And tolerance toward the faith convictions of others is a good thing. But sloppiness of conviction is an entirely different matter. Religious traditions and meanings cannot be served up in a holy smorgasbord so that spiritual consumers can reach for a bit of this and a bit of that.

Today we seem to have no authority for belief, no reference point against which to evaluate positive or negative faith. Orthodoxy is taken to mean whatever we want or need. It is certainly true that we must personalize faith. If it is not personalized, then faith is never truly owned. But as Christians we must ultimately integrate and evaluate our own personal beliefs (1) against the Scriptures, (2) against the doctrines of our own faith community, and (3) against the heritage and theology of the universal church.

The doctrine of the priesthood of all believers, held by the free churches, affirms that no person or hierarchy has authority over the content of another person's faith. It exhibits a tolerance for personal interpretation and individual expression of faith. But this doctrine does not give persons the *right* to believe whatever they want to believe. Rather, the emphasis is upon the *responsibility* to interpret faithfully the Scripture. Many people in the churches have misunderstood the relationship between right and responsibility.

It does matter who God is to you. It does matter whether faith has depth. It does matter whether your faith, as I have heard Ernst Campbell say, "knows the simplicity on the far side of complexity, rather than becomes satisfied with the simplicity on the near side of complexity." Or, to repeat the words of Bishop Stephen Neill, the challenge of faith is always to "commit all that you know of yourself, to all that you know of God." A faith that is growing and maturing is undoubtedly the strongest force for good in the world. A faith that is simplistic, naive, or uninformed is dangerous. The tragic death of hundreds at the Jonestown colony is substantiation enough of that fact.

The opposite of faith is not doubt but apathy. Doubt and faith are both active processes in building a deep and lasting foundation for life. There is a tug and pull between doubt and faith. Faith satisfies and doubt dissatisfies. Faith brings life into perspective, and doubt jostles it out of perspective. Before we allow faith to satisfy at too early or superficial a stage, doubt is needed to provide the corrective. In a "becoming" Christian, doubt and faith interplay throughout an entire lifetime.

A typical belief for a junior high Christian might be that God cures illness when you pray. So when her favorite grandmother becomes ill, the young person prays for health and healing. When the grandmother dies, the youth is caught in a faith crisis, often blaming either God or herself. The youth's faith is partially correct: God is involved in life, its healing, and its death. But it is much too simplistic to believe that if we pray, everyone will become well. Such a belief puts us, and not God, in the driver's seat. When doubt is encouraged, the young person can get a better perspective on that belief and eventually deepen her faith. If not, the young person could turn from God as being unfaithful or worry that she did not pray often enough or well enough. Guilt might be carried for years. A faith clarifier could lead the young person into doubt and, in doing so, provide a crucial faith-shaping role.

The faith of many youth is joyful, superficial, and emotional. There are appropriate times simply to let them be and let them enjoy that level of "faith-experiencing." The faith they have claimed is not yet ready to be deepened. But there are also times to challenge their faith, to lead them into creative doubt, and thus deepen the reservoir of their experience, their theology, and their world view.

Doubt is the tool that carries us to the edge of our convictions and to the frontiers of new possibilities. It can be a positive and helpful influence upon our faith. For youth, doubt can often be a corrective to sweeping generalizations, extremism, or simplifications. "Extremism is an inherent danger to the young. When we are young, we get a piece of the truth, and we think we have all the truth. . . . The less we know, the easier it is to convince ourselves that we know everything." [1]

We need both to accept the faith of young people for what it is and to challenge them to greater depths. It is imperative that they feel the acceptance and the challenge together. We must not convey the impression "Your beliefs are not good enough" nor "Your beliefs are sufficient." Rather, we must say, "I affirm where you are spiritually. I encourage you to deepen your faith even more," or "Your faith is fulfilling you now. But look how much more awaits you!"

We need also to note that it is not at all uncommon to find adolescents who enjoy a deep, provocative faith that is vibrant and alive and instigates growth in the adults and youth around them.

The longer young persons freeze faith development at an immature level, the more likely it is that their faith will be discarded in young adulthood or that their level of faith will be arrested and will never plunge to a more mature level.

A strong definition of sin includes the arrest of our development toward God either in understanding, in our personal will, in our actions, or in our relationship with God. Immature faith not only lacks its own rewards, but it is also against God's will and way. God created us as becomers, as developmental beings. The apostle Paul says, "Do not be like children in your thinking, my brothers; be children so far as evil is concerned, but be grown up in your thinking" (1 Corinthians 14:20, TEV). Or again, "As a matter of fact, my brothers, I could not talk to you as I talk to people who have the Spirit; I had to talk to you as though you belonged to this world, as children in the Christian faith. I had to feed you milk, not solid food, because you were not ready for it" (1 Corinthians 3:1-2a, TEV).

Criteria of Faith Quality

If we were going to develop a "quality control" for faith, what criteria would we use? That is another way of asking, "What do we expect of our faith?" "What should it do for us?" As we help young people grow in the faith and as we are concerned (as they are concerned)

[1] William H. Willimon, *The Gospel for the Person Who Has Everything* (Valley Forge: Judson Press, 1978), p. 42.

that their faith be an expression of maturity, we need some criteria against which to evaluate that faith.

I would suggest, as a beginning toward that goal, the following nine statements. If a young person could respond positively to these statements about his or her faith, he or she would have a maturing faith indeed. Areas where a person is less sure would be areas where more reflection is needed.

MY FAITH . . .

	DEFINITELY YES				DEFINITELY NO		
1. *is personally satisfying.* (I enjoy it; it's a source of satisfaction.)	1	2	3	4	5	6	7
2. *nourishes me personally and stimulates my growth.* (It's always renewing and challenging me.)	1	2	3	4	5	6	7
3. *offers helpful external resources.* (It brings help to me from the outside; from God, from other people, from the Bible or books, etc.)	1	2	3	4	5	6	7
4. *places me in touch with others' needs.* (These needs might be physical, emotional, spiritual.)	1	2	3	4	5	6	7
5. *makes me able to interpret life's experiences.* (It helps me understand my feelings and experiences.)	1	2	3	4	5	6	7
6. *makes me able to be open to the new.* (I can face new situations because of my faith.)	1	2	3	4	5	6	7

MY FAITH . . .	DEFINITELY YES				DEFINITELY NO		
	1	2	3	4	5	6	7

7. *causes me to realize my personal potential.*
   (My faith helps me understand my future; to know my talents and gifts; to become a better person.)   1 2 3 4 5 6 7

8. *causes me to be selflessly humble.*
   (I think of others first; I realize my own limitations.)   1 2 3 4 5 6 7

9. *changes from year to year.*
   (It grows and deepens as I become older.)   1 2 3 4 5 6 7

Another way to evaluate faith would be to describe qualities of immature faith.

IMMATURE FAITH CAN BE CHARACTERIZED BY . . .

1. *too strong a need for certainty.* Not all questions can be answered; the word ''faith'' implies that one cannot know everything; mature faith can live comfortably with some uncertainty.

2. *too small a view of God.* No one can know everything about God or always know God's expectations for one's life; often ideas of God are too small, too limiting, too self-serving.

3. *self-centeredness.* An immature faith seeks only a reward for oneself; centers too exclusively upon one's own personal needs.

4. *it being used as a crutch, an excuse, a comfort.* In all such cases faith is in the way of personal growth and development.

5. *a lack of surprises or challenges.* Vibrant faith often makes surprising demands upon one. It confronts one where one least expects it.

6. *a one-time faith decision rather than a lifelong journey.* Immature faith lets the believer think that he or she has ''made it,'' that one is on the inside while others are on the outside; it refuses to see faith as a lifelong series of decisions and stages.

7. *a structure of beliefs rather than a responsiveness of faith.* A person holds fast to a set of theological beliefs and thinks of faith as a collection of carefully selected convictions rather than seeing faith as more fluid and dynamic, more responsive to the divine relationship.

8. *a privatized rather than a personalized focus.* A private faith has no interests in being shared with others; a personalized faith is deeply personal, but it is also shared in relationships.

9. *an institutional rather than a corporate concern.* A faith that gives ultimate allegiance to an institution, i.e., a church, is not the same as a faith that binds one to a corporate body of believers.

What Is a Person of Christian Faith?

A person of Christian faith embodies a love that is both free and accountable.

When we first encounter the Christian faith, we experience a love that is freely given—God's grace to us. But as we accept this freely given love, we become aware of another dimension of God's love. We walk around this love and see it from the back. The back side of this free love of God is what God expects of us—accountable love with its responsibilities. As we consider both the front side and the back side of the gospel message, we will recognize ways in which we have distorted this message.

The front side of the gospel message is grace. The headline of our faith is a free, gracious love from God that we do not deserve and cannot earn. This *free love* makes the statement, "I love you regardless of what you do to return my love." When we are loved regardless of the consequences, that love is both free and freeing.

But rather than *love that frees,* most of us satisfy ourselves with *love that cheapens. Cheap love* is superficial love. Jealous and conditional love is cheap love. Relationships where we have to prove ourselves, where we are not valued or prized, are characteristic of love that we feel we must earn—cheap love. We all have so much cheap love in each of our lives that we prize highly those precious few relationships built on the free love that accepts us as we are.

The back side of the Christian message carries the implications of *free love,* that is, *accountable love.* Accountable love is love that cares.

Accountable love is a love that motivates us to hold onto one another, to call one another to growth and maturity. Therefore, accountable love renews and vitalizes all of our lives. It is a love with faithfulness, with eternity as the clock that measures its duration. But most of us distort *accountable love* into *careless love,* where nothing is expected and no strings are ever attached. It is love with no requirements—fleeting love—love of the moment. Such a careless love makes no difference and holds no meaning.

If we accept God's *free love,* the implications are that we must enter into a relationship with God that has accountability. We will then be held accountable by God in love.

THE FRONT SIDE OF THE GOSPEL

FREE LOVE VS. CHEAP LOVE

THE BACK SIDE OF THE GOSPEL

ACCOUNTABLE LOVE VS. CARELESS LOVE

When we join together the front side of the gospel, *free love* (love that accepts me as I am), with the back side of the gospel, *accountable love* (love that binds and secures), then we have a *free and accountable love that is the whole of the gospel.* God is calling us to a love that frees, on the one hand, and holds us to our commitments, on the other hand.

But how sad it is that so many of our homes, so many of our families, so many of our churches are built around cheap love on the front side and careless love on the back side. People feel neither accepted nor cared for. Many people do not feel accepted by God because they think only good or better people are really accepted by God. And they are not bound to God because they're frightened of that much responsibility or commitment.

Accountable Love

Our whole society today is running from accountable love—lovers who choose to live together; friends who refuse to challenge one another; parents who won't provide helpful limits for their children; or church members who run scared the minute the word "commitment" is mentioned. We appear absolutely enamored with *careless love!* We don't want to inconvenience anyone; we don't want to make mutual demands upon anyone; we don't want to place expectations in anyone's path.

The younger generation is frequently charged with shirking accountability. But this problem does not belong only to those on the high school or college campus. Those of us in the pulpit and pew and those of today's older generation are just as guilty. Anytime I hear a senior adult say that he or she is too old to sit in the crib room and hold a baby or that he or she has taken a turn with the second graders and now it's someone else's turn, I know I'm hearing from a senior adult caught up in careless love. Whenever I see someone who lives in a lovely home, with lovely cars and the nicest clothes, but not sharing a sacrificial percentage of her or his income toward helping others, I know I'm seeing a person caught by the grip of careless love. We are all guilty—it is symptomatic of our age.

Accountable love is perhaps more difficult to comprehend. Let me use an illustration from my own ministry with youth. Accountable love was the unexpected "theme" of one youth retreat.

I had taken a group of youth to a lodge that was in a remote location. At 10:00 P.M. the second night out, two boyfriends unexpectedly drove up to meet two girl friends who were in the senior high group. And we had an instant problem! The boys had graduated from high school six months before. During high school they had been an active part of our youth fellowship group. But these capable young men, in all ways able to enter the adult world, seemed stalled in their willingness to face the post-high-school decisions of life.

The counselors huddled soon after their arrival to decide what to do. What was the loving thing to do? If we let them stay overnight, we would not be encouraging their forward momentum to maturity. If we sent them home, we would no doubt anger the girls and the boys.

Accountability was really the question. Should we risk anger, alienation, and misunderstanding? Was it more important to hold them accountable for their own actions? For me, the issue was really even more complicated than that. I had played the role of close friend and near-father to these boys. For five years, I had appreciated and enjoyed their friendships. I knew that if I sent them home, my contact with them and their relationship with the church might come to an end. My own feelings and emotions were involved.

Midnight rolled around and the boys were not moving. The adults finally had to take action. We decided to take the risk and hold the boys accountable for their actions. How painful it was for me to see the looks on their faces, not only that night, but for weeks and months to come, of surprise, of distrust, of hurt, and of anger! They wondered out loud, "How can a friend of ours treat us this way? How can you kick us out?" I wondered back, out loud, "How can someone who loves you treat you any other way?"

In the cab of a pickup truck at three in the morning with a blizzard of snow falling about us, I shared with them my disappointment during the past six months and my strong belief in their future if they would believe in it themselves. I can only hope that someday they will look back on that occasion and thank a group of adults who loved them enough to hold them accountable. Lesser love would have found an easier solution.

In the short run it *appears* much easier to be friends without holding one another mutually accountable. It *appears* much easier to rear your children without truly holding them accountable. It *appears* easier to be in a church that cannot or will not hold you accountable. And it is certainly much easier to follow a "god" who does not seem to hold you accountable.

In the story of Ananias and Sapphira in Acts they, too, thought it to be much easier to avoid accountability.

They were a part of the first Christian community. The members of this community entered a covenant with their God. They were to be loyal to God, and God was to be loyal to them. It was a mutual vow of accountable love. This first church felt led of God to establish that if any member sold a property, the proceeds of that property would be given to the church so that the common ministry could be furthered. But Ananias decided to go only halfway. He sold his property and gave only part of it to the church. He and his wife kept back the rest. They broke the church's covenant. In this story we often get overly concerned with their punishment. Both of them denied their wrongdoing, and both of them came under conviction and fell over dead. But we miss the real point when we accent the punishment. The point is, rather, that the early church expected that their love for each other and for God would be an accountable love, love filled with enough concern and seriousness that it would be binding, not a casual or flippant love. The story is not about the cruelty of their punishment but of the seriousness of the church's love.

In healthy circumstances, to be held accountable means that someone will help me keep my life on the track that I have chosen. Mutual accountability with a group means that together we are going to be responsible to keep our common goals on target.

We use the words "*holding* another person accountable," and there's something very loving about holding another person. When we take someone into our arms, when we hold, touch, embrace, reach out to another—these are expressions of love.

Indeed to care enough in a loving relationship to hold someone accountable reflects a love that is deep, abiding, and true. A group of people, if they are truly serious with one another, will hold one another accountable in love.

One of the most important persons in my life was a man named Mr. Ward. Mr. Ward was a speech and drama teacher in my high school. He was the town philosopher and the village radical in my little community in central Missouri.

Few men have had more impact upon my life. He would start every semester with a new class by scaring the wits out of us with all the commitments and expectations that he had for us. He would tell us how seriously he would hold us accountable. And he would end the class by saying that if anyone felt he or she could not live up to the expectations, the person should get up and leave. But then he would say, "But if you really want to be challenged, if you truly want to think, then I'll promise all my efforts to that end." No one would ever leave the class, but it did sufficiently scare us to death.

And Mr. Ward followed up on his promise. He truly cared about his students. He cared about our troubles that had nothing to do with speech or drama. I can still remember him saying to me, on numerous occasions, "Steve, I believe in you. I count on you." And through his love, I felt free to think and grow as I had never done before.

Mr. Ward's love and accountability were a great deal like the accountable love that God has for us. Yes, we're challenged and frightened with the expectations that God has for us. Yet God doesn't force us to accept such love. God offers it. God is saying to us, "If you decide to enter into covenant with me, to be my faithful people in your homes, with your children, in your work, with your friends, in your school—wherever you might be, your life will take on a richer meaning that you cannot now imagine. You will taste freedom. You will be taking my love as seriously as I am taking you.''

That is God's promise to us.

Free Love

What a gift—what an incredible gift is God's free love! Just as parents love their child regardless of whether the child returns the love or regardless of the child's actions or behavior, so much more does our heavenly Parent love us, regardless of whether we love back or whether we deserve the love.

A love that we can freely accept or a love that we must earn—that is the choice which Jesus clearly offers. Each love had its own ethic. The ethic of grace is an ethic of natural response because our actions are in response to God's first action toward us. ''We love, because he first loved us.''

The ethic of a love which we must earn is an ethic of achievement. Our actions are intended to achieve a certain status with God. We act in order to please, in order to gain acceptance. Many Christians have never fully realized the extraordinary difference which the reality of grace can make. Grace should be the first chapter of the faith which we advocate to youth. It is the reality most suited to their developmental needs.

ETHIC OF RESPONSE	ETHIC OF ACHIEVEMENT
(We love because God first loved us.)	(We love in order to gain status with God.)
Motivation: Gratitude	*Motivation: Obligation*
We act regardless of whether we win or lose.	We act in order to get results, to be successful or victorious.
We serve because we know that we are loved and accepted.	We serve in order to gain love and acceptance.
We aim toward doing the maximum.	We aim toward doing the minimum.

Summary

There is no gospel that young people need to hear more clearly than the gospel of a free and accountable love. We have too exclusively taught youth that everything they want in life they must earn. There is one thing in life that they do not have to earn and cannot possibly earn, and that is God's love (Ephesians 2:8-9). God loves each young person regardless of what a person does or does not do in return. Each is accepted just as each one is. What good news that is for an adolescent: to be thoroughly and unconditionally accepted—by God, no less!

But that is only half the picture. Youth also need to know of God's accountable love. They need to know that God wants to enter into a relationship that will be taken seriously. It will be a relationship where promises are taken seriously, where *they* as persons are taken seriously. They will come to know that God has great hopes and a tremendous purpose for their lives. And that, in love, God will hold them accountable for what they make of life's possibilities.

The front side and the back side of the gospel—a free and accountable love—are what it means to be a person of Christian faith today. Young people who begin to grasp this gospel are well on their way to mature faith and fullness of life.

Jesus is the example of that kind of love incarnated. Through his life we can see a human example of a free and accountable love at work. Yet most children and youth of the church have an almost nonexistent sense of Jesus' humanity. In liberal and conservative churches alike, we pour layers of doctrine and theology over Jesus' humanity as to make him barely distinguishable. We so stress the divine, sinless, perfect, meek, and mild Lord of faith that our young people have no knowledge of the earthy, troubled, worried, joyful, caring, revolutionary Jesus of history.

It is the *man* that youth should see first. Let them come to know Jesus as a person who treated women as equals, who lost his cool in the temple, who humbled himself to wash the feet of others and who exalted himself on Palm Sunday, who celebrated with wine at a wedding, who played with children, who disobeyed his parents at age twelve, who was frightened in Gethsemane, who offended his townspeople in Nazareth, and who held intimate friendships with Mary, Martha, and Lazarus. Let them see Jesus as a man first!

Then, we can interpret to them the role Jesus played in history, the special idea of incarnation and the new relationship made possible with God for each of us. We need more of a beginnings approach to Jesus and less of a basics style.

Youth need to identify with Jesus. They need to feel his feelings with him; to walk his steps with him; to identify with his words and thoughts; to watch him as he grew! When they meet this Jesus, they will meet a compelling and appealing expression of free and accountable love in raw flesh and real blood!

Chapter 10

A New Mandate!

The challenge of faith shaping with youth remains a diffused agenda in far too many homes and churches. Let us not avoid what is intangible just because it cannot be easily seen or scientifically charted. From Hebrews we are reminded, "Faith is the substance of things hoped for, the evidence of things not seen" (11:1, KJV). Following this biblical advice, we need to help youth discover the very substance of their hopes!

The act of welcoming youth into the faith deserves our most creative and determined response. We must not be guilty of forcing faith upon youth, but, rather, we must surround them with positive faith-shaping experiences in a variety of the settings of their lives.

The task of faith shaping by persons in their adolescent and young adult years is sacred and holy. We must allow it to happen along God's timetable. Our efforts will, it is hoped, transmit an enticement toward faith and not anxiousness about faith.

Although it has not been stated as such, this is without apology a book on personal evangelism. It expresses an evangelistic concern to share faith with adolescents and young adults.

This approach has attempted to overcome the two ways we have often exclusively expressed our evangelistic concern for youth. This exclusivity is reflected when we care only for the first-time decision of faith and not the lifelong journey of faith. Secondly, it is reflected when evangelism is narrowly defined as an activity of directness but not also of nearness.

If we are to speak an inclusive evangelistic message to the youth in our homes and churches, then the "words" we use will have to be EMBODIED WORDS as well as SPOKEN WORDS. We will have to live the message as well as verbalize it. We will need to be more concerned that youth come to *their* own saving knowledge of Christ than to *our* saving knowledge of Christ.

We are challenged in both the Old and New Testaments with a significant mandate to share the precious "words" of faith with our youth.

Hear now these words of Scripture:

THE OLD TESTAMENT MANDATE FOR FAITH NURTURING

"Israel, remember this! The Lord—and the Lord alone—is our God. Love the Lord your God with all your heart, with all your soul, and with all your strength. Never forget these commands that I am giving you today. *Teach them to your children and youth.* Repeat them when you are at home and when you are away, when you are resting and when you are working. Tie them on your arms and wear them on your foreheads as a reminder. Write them on the doorposts of your houses and on your gates.

"In times to come your *children and youth* will ask you, 'Why did the Lord our God command us to obey all these laws?' Then tell them, 'We were slaves of the king of Egypt, and the Lord rescued us by his great power. With our own eyes we saw him work miracles . . .'" (Deuteronomy 6:4-9, 20-22*a*, TEV; the term "children" is made inclusive of youth in the two italicized sections by the author).

When young persons eventually ask, at their point of readiness, "Why does God call us to faith?" answer them not with doctrine or creed, but share with them the story of our faith and the story of our biblical heritage. Show them God acting in human lives, interrupting history with divine loving concern. Through these stories they will most fully come to faith.

THE NEW TESTAMENT MANDATE FOR FAITH NURTURING

> "If our gift be the stimulating of the faith of others let us set ourselves to it" (Romans 12:8a, Phillips).

If the gift has been freely given to us;

if the opportunity to use the gift afforded us;

if the need is felt to be genuine; then surely this is a personal calling from God. Young persons today, as much as ever before, need gifted and committed persons who see as their calling the nurturing of the adolescent faith journey.

The work of this book can only be a beginning, a send-off, a challenge, a mandate! Now, as these pages come to an end, our real "work" begins as we commit ourselves anew to create the environment, establish the priorities, and develop the relationships that will authentically speak God's evangelistic message of concern to young persons.

If we give adolescent faith nurturing our finest efforts and most prayerful concern, then persons of mature Christian faith will emerge. And when our young people receive and shape such a faith, we will be living our finest hour!

Appendix

Christian Discipleship Journey

**The First Baptist Church,
Dayton, Ohio**

**. . . INFORMATION SHEET . . .   Junior High Youth
1980 January**

DO YOU WANT TO GO ON A JOURNEY???

*Who wouldn't? Everyone enjoys journeys and trips, particularly
to faraway or unusual places . . . like Hawaii, or Disney World, or
Europe, or Hong Kong, or . . . well, you could let your mind run wild
with the excitement of a long journey!*

The Christian Discipleship Journey is an exciting journey, too! It will
be a journey where you can also travel great distances, but not in miles.
This is a journey with your life: to discover what *possibilities for you*
there are in the Christian life!

You will find yourself in the midst of all kinds of experiences on this journey, but it's like any other journey: if you don't jump into it completely, you probably won't enjoy yourself. (Hawaii wouldn't be much fun if you just sat in your hotel room!) When you decide to take this journey, make certain it is your choice and your decision. Make certain you want to discover some answers to this question:

Am I ready to consider the Christian journey for my life?

This journey is for all junior high youth. Your decision to be baptized or to join the church is not really dependent on this journey, although what you learn here should help you down the road of Christian discipleship, and it might help you make the important decision of accepting God into your life.

If you are interested, study the covenant and information enclosed. We're just about to pack up and begin!

ROAD MAP

Just like any trip, you're going to have to know what to plan for and how and where you're going to travel. Here's a Road Map for the Christian Discipleship Journey:

1. *One parent (or substitute) accompanies each young person in the Journey.*
2. *Each young person is teamed with one parent (not one's own), and these teams are partners for the Journey.*
3. *Each adult-youth team "covenants" to arrive at one of the destinations of the Journey by February 10, 1980.*
4. *In each destination there will be some required and some optional projects. The projects must be the work of the youth, but the adults are to be supportive in the completion of each project. Projects that have an asterisk (*) beside them are projects in which two or more youth in the Journey can work together.*
5. *You will be given folders in which to record your progress and reactions.*

Overall Requirements for All Journeyers

(1) Attend the overnight retreat without parents. This is a concept-building session on the discipleship concepts of "belonging" and "believing," especially designed for junior high youth.

(2) Attend the work session, at midpoint in the journey, with your adult partner, and attend a Review Session with your adult partner and a deacon on the last day of the journey.

Schedule of Group Gatherings for the 1980 Journey

Friday,	January 4,	6:00 P.M.	Youth and Parents Dinner and Organizational Meeting
		8:00 P.M.	Youth only leave for Camp Kirkwood overnight retreat
Saturday,	January 5,	5:00 P.M.	Youth return to the church
Sunday,	January 27,	12:30 P.M.	Light lunch at church after church school
			Youth and Parent Partner Work Session: midway point
Sunday,	February 10,	11:15 A.M.	Youth and Parent Partners each meet privately with one deacon to review completed work and affirm the journey
		12:30 P.M.	Congregational recognition of youth who have completed their destination; Presentation of Christian Discipleship Journey certificates

Destination: Bible and Belief

REQUIRED:

1. Read the booklet "The Bible and Me" and answer questions at the end of the book. Also read our new Church Covenant. Answer questions on Sheet A.
2. Lead your family in daily devotions for one week using *The Secret Place,* a small magazine available at the church.

3. Interview your adult partner on the meaning of prayer in his/her life. Write down five questions you wish to ask and record the answers.

OPTIONALS:
(Choose 2)

1. Create a Bible story pantomime or skit for a group of junior highs to perform during the church school hour for another class. Selection of this Bible story should be coordinated with the teacher.
2. Read *Pilgrim's Progress,* written by an early Baptist pastor, John Bunyan, and answer questions related to the book on Sheet B.
3. Memorize Matthew 5:1-12 or 1 Corinthians 13.
4. Write a short paper on the "Five Identifying Marks" of a Christian. Base this on your own opinion.
5. Read Matthew 4:23–5:16 in each of the following translations: *The Living Bible, The New English Bible,* Today's English Version, the King James Version, and the Revised Standard Version. Write on a sheet or record on a tape recorder what you think this passage is saying and your reactions from reading it in the different translations.

Destination: Serving and Caring

REQUIRED:

* 1. Complete two hours in mission to the community through projects of the Community Mission committee of our Board of Mission.
2. Visit one "shut-in" church member in that person's home or a nursing home, and take something that you have made to affirm that you care, such as cookies, a potted plant, a card, a craft item.

3. Recycle cans, glass, newspaper, and aluminum in your home for three weeks and deliver items to a recycling center, or spend two hours on a litter hike in your neighborhood.

OPTIONALS:
(Choose 2)

* 1. Complete one project from the Service Projects booklet of the American Baptist Churches, U.S.A.
2. Read the booklet entitled "Love" and answer related questions on Sheet E.
3. Read a book and answer related questions on Sheet F (biographical or missionary/ prophet: Martin Luther King, Jr., Albert Schweitzer, Tom Dooley). You may use the book *Baptists Who Dared*.
4. Accompany the deacons as they serve Communion in homes to shut-ins on one Sunday afternoon.
5. Find three Bible verses that encourage God's people to care for the world, to be good stewards of what God has given us. Select one of these verses that would make an attractive "paper banner." You can get a long roll of paper from the church, and use felt-tip pens or tempera paint.

Destination: Baptists and Heritage

REQUIRED:

* 1. Attend one other American Baptist church for worship.
* 2. Attend a church of another denomination for worship one Sunday.
3. Read the book *The New Disciple* by Joseph and Arline Ban and answer related questions on Sheet C.
4. Read *The Story of American Baptists*. Answer the questions on Sheet D.

OPTIONALS:
(Choose 1)

1. Write a letter to one American Baptist international missionary telling him/her

who you are, about your discipleship journey, and offering a short prayer for their
work.

2. American Baptists have two ordinances:
   baptism and Communion. Using resource
   books, answer these questions:
   Where did baptism begin? When do Baptists baptize people? What is our form of
   baptism called? Why do we baptize in the
   way that we do? What do we think that
   baptism means? What are other forms of
   baptisms that other churches use?
   Why do we celebrate the Lord's Supper?
   Where did this practice begin? What does
   the bread and the juice symbolize? What
   is the symbolism of "sitting at the table
   of the Lord"? According to American
   Baptists, who can sit at the Lord's table?

3. Make a time line tracing the beginning of
   the Baptist denomination, ending with the
   present-day American Baptist Churches,
   U.S.A.

4. Make a large poster stating the major beliefs of Baptists.

Destination: The Local Church

REQUIRED:

1. Complete the 1980 Pledge Card and turn
   it in if you haven't.

* 2. Attend the January 30 annual meeting of
   the congregation.

3. Complete the Christian Stewardship Audit
   based upon your life-style. Write a short
   prayer on the back side based upon the
   signs in your life of being God's steward.

4. Read the booklet "A Sesquicentennial
   History of First Baptist Church, Dayton,
   Ohio" and answer related questions on
   Sheet G.

OPTIONALS: * 1. Attend the Martin Luther King, Jr., Com-
(Choose 3)   munity Birthday Observance worship ser-
                          vice on Tuesday, January 15, 7:30 P.M.
                          Answer related questions on Sheet H.
                    2. Write a prayer that you will give as the
                       invocation in a worship service on Sun-
                       day.
                    3. Memorize our church covenant.
                    4. Create a bulletin board in one of the chil-
                       dren's church school classes based on a
                       theme they are currently studying.
                    5. Interview a long-time church member and
                       write a one-page description of his or her
                       experiences within our church.
                    6. Help in a children's church school class
                       for two Sundays.
                    7. Take pictures (you may borrow the church's
                       Polaroid from the Resource Center if you
                       need it) of scenes around the church de-
                       picting:
                       —the church at play
                       —the worshiping church
                       —the church where people pray to-
                         gether
                       —the singing church
                       —the church, a place to learn
                       —the church, a place where youth are
                         accepted
                       —the church for all ages

On poster paper, mount these pictures with their captions. Put a title
on your display that you think describes the church.

*The Youth Ministry Committee is responsible for administering the
Christian Discipleship Journey. Deacons will review the progress of
each participant and give congregational recognition for those who
complete their stage of the Journey.*

(